COOL GUIDE
New York

teNeues

Imprint

Editors: Martin Nicholas Kunz

Editorial coordination: Katharina Feuer, Ariane Preusch, Manuela Roth

Photos (location): Roland Bauer (Dean & DeLuca, MoMA Design and Book Store, moss, 45rpm); © Ago, © Merkato 55, © Eric Laignel for Nobu 57, © Pop Burger, © 230 Fifth, © Cielo, © Kiss and Fly, © Marquee, © Gramercy Park Hotel (Rose Bar & Jade Bar), © ABC Carpet & Home, © Patricia Field, © Takashimaya; Claudia Hehr (Balthazar, Katz's Delicatessen, La Esquina, Apple Store 5th Avenue, Strand Bookstore, American Museum of Natural History, Coney Island, The Cloisters Museum and Gardens, Statue of Liberty); Eisenhart Keimeyer (Ago, Blue Water Grill, Café Sabarsky, Matsugen, Philippe Chow, APT, BIJOUX, Cellar Bar, Fat Black Pussycat, de Vera, UNIQLO, Brooklyn Bridge); Martin Nicholas Kunz (Keens Steakhouse, Peasant, Spice Market, The Mercer Kitchen, F·A·O Schwarz, Tribeca Issey Miyake, Brooklyn Bridge, Bryant Park, The Skyscraper Museum, Times Square, Top of the Rock Observation Deck)

Cover photo (location): Martin Nicholas Kunz (Times Square)

Back cover photos from top to bottom (location): Eisenhart Keimeyer (APT, UNIQLO), Martin Nicholas Kunz (Brooklyn Bridge), Michelle Galindo (Spice Market)

Price categories: $ = reasonable, $$ = moderate, $$$ = upscale, $$$$ = expensive

Introduction: Patrice Farameh

Layout & Pre-press, Imaging: fusion publishing, Jan Hausberg

Translations: Übersetzungsbüro RR Communications: German: Jasmin Klück, Romina Russo; French: Caroline Crepieux, Félicien Guebane; Spanish: Sylvia Lyschik, Sergio Ramos

Produced by fusion publishing GmbH, Berlin   www.fusion-publishing.com

Published by teNeues Publishing Group

teNeues Verlag Gmbh + Co. KG
Am Selder 37
47906 Kempen, Germany
Tel.: 0049-(0)2152-916-0
Fax: 0049-(0)2152-916-111
E-mail: books@teneues.de

teNeues Publishing Company
16 West 22nd Street
New York, NY 10010, USA
Tel.: 001-212-627-9090
Fax: 001-212-627-9511

teNeues Publishing UK Ltd.
York Villa, York Road
Byfleet
KT14 7HX, Great Britain
Tel.: 0044-1932-403509
Fax: 0044-1932-403514

teNeues France S.A.R.L.
93, rue Bannier
45000 Orléans, France
Tel.: 0033-2-38541071
Fax: 0033-2-38625340

Press department: arehn@teneues.de
Tel.: 0049-2152-916-202

www.teneues.com

ISBN: 978-3-8327-9293-0

© 2008 teNeues Verlag GmbH + Co. KG, Kempen

Printed in Italy

Bibliographic information published by the Deutsche Nationalbibliothek.
The Deutsche Nationalbibliothek lists this publication in the Deutsche Nationalbibliografie;
detailed bibliographic data are available on the Internet at http://dnb.d-nb.de.

RESTAURANTS & CAFÉS

CLUBS, LOUNGES & BARS

SHOPS

HIGHLIGHTS

SERVICE

Introduction

There is no debate that New York City is the epitome of cool. This metropolis of bright lights that never stops is one of the most beloved cities in the world, and for good reason. From the spectacular illuminating skyline to the multi-ethnic neighborhoods, New York City is the incubator for fresh concepts in dining, sleeping, entertaining, and flirting. Even a leisurely tour through its assorted neighborhoods and boroughs is an adventure in itself. Whether it is as iconic as a trip to the looming Statue of Liberty or taking in all the glory of the hustle and bustle of city life sitting in Bryant Park, there is a great diversity of places to explore and immerse oneself in the true New York spirit.

Not only fit for fashionistas and trendsetters, New York is also home to some of the most innovative chefs and restaurateurs with award-winning cuisine in undoubtedly the most glamorous settings. A lunch in the city might mean a towering seafood plate of lobster and oysters in the cozy French bakery and bistro Balthazar or a bite of a designer mini-burger served in a luxuriously retro setting at Pop Burger.

With its top-rated restaurants, super chic boutiques, and ultra-hip international scene, New York City has continually defined what is cool for the rest of the nation as the Big Apple of the world's eye.

Patrice Farameh

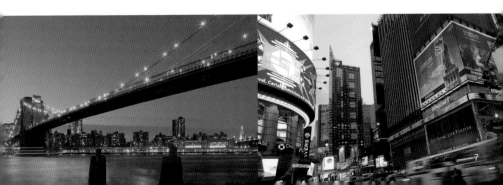

7

Einleitung

Es steht außer Frage, dass New York City der Inbegriff von „cool" ist. Diese Metropole der hellen Lichter, die niemals schläft, ist eine der beliebtesten Städte der Welt, und das aus gutem Grund. Von der spektakulär beleuchteten Skyline bis hin zu den multiethnischen Vierteln ist New York City der Brutkasten für eine neue Auffassung von Essen, Schlafen, Unterhaltung und Flirten. Selbst ein gemächlicher Spaziergang durch die verschiedenen Viertel und Bezirke ist schon ein Abenteuer für sich. Ob man nun einen Ausflug mit Kultcharakter zur über die Stadt herausragenden Freiheitsstatue unternimmt oder ganz einfach im Bryant Park sitzt und das herrlich geschäftige Treiben des Stadtlebens auf sich wirken lässt – es gibt viele verschiedene Flecken zu entdecken, an denen man in den wahren Geist New Yorks eintauchen kann.

New York ist nicht nur der richtige Platz für Modefans und Trendsetter, sondern auch das Zuhause einiger der innovativsten Chefköche und Gastronome, die ihre preisgekrönte Küche in den zweifellos schicksten Ambienten präsentieren. Ein Mittagessen in der Stadt könnte eine riesige Fischplatte mit Hummern und Austern im gemütlichen französischen Bäckerei-Bistro Balthazar sein, ebenso wie ein Bissen eines Designer-Miniburgers, der bei Pop Burger in einem luxuriösen Retro-Ambiente serviert wird.

Mit seinen als erstklassig bewerteten Restaurants, den superschicken Boutiquen und der hypermodernen internationalen Szene hat New York, der Big Apple, stets vorgegeben, was für den Rest des Landes *cool* ist.

Patrice Farameh

Introduction

La question ne se pose pas, New York est l'incarnation de la vie « cool ». Cette métropole aux lumières étincelantes qui ne dort jamais est une des villes les plus appréciées au monde, et pour cause. De son panorama spectaculaire à ses quartiers multiethniques, New York est un véritable vivier de concepts nouveaux dans les domaines de la gastronomie, de l'hôtellerie, du divertissement et des rencontres amoureuses. Une simple promenade tranquille dans les différents quartiers et arrondissements est une aventure en soi. Que ce soit pour visiter la classique Statue de la liberté ou observer l'effervescence de la vie citadine assis tranquillement dans Bryant Park, il y a une multitude d'endroits à explorer pour s'immerger dans le vrai esprit de New York.

On ne trouve pas que des victimes de la mode et des faiseurs de mode, New York est aussi le foyer de nombreux chefs et restaurateurs innovants, avec une cuisine reconnue dans un environnement très glamour. Un déjeuner en ville pourra se transformer en un gigantesque plateau de fruits de mer avec de la langouste et des huitres dans le confortable bistro français Balthazar ou en une bouchée de mini-burger servi dans un décor rétro-luxe au Pop Burger.

Avec ses restaurants très cotés, ses boutiques super chics et sa scène ultra internationale, New York City, la plus « Grosse pomme » du monde a toujours su donner le ton en terme de « cool » pour le reste du pays.

Patrice Farameh

Introducción

No cabe duda de que Nueva York es sinónimo de lo nuevo, lo moderno y lo impactante. La metrópoli de luces cegadoras que nunca duerme es una de las ciudades más aclamadas en todo el mundo –y con motivo. Desde la espectacular silueta luminosa dibujada en el horizonte hasta sus barrios multiétnicos, Nueva York se revela como un caldo de cultivo de nuevas tendencias gastronómicas, hoteleras, del ocio y del arte del cortejo. Incluso un paseo tranquilo por sus diversos barrios y distritos puede convertirse en toda una aventura. Hay tantos lugares por descubrir como posibilidades para sumergirse en el verdadero espíritu de Nueva York; bien sea a través de una excursión de carácter icónico a la imponente Estatua de la Libertad o simplemente disfrutando y absorbiendo todo el esplendor de la vida bulliciosa de esta gran urbe sentado en el parque Bryant.

Esta ciudad no sólo atrae a los adeptos a la moda y a aquellos que marcan tendencias, sino que también es el hogar de algunos de los cocineros y gastrónomos más innovadores, que ofrecen sus galardonados platos en entornos revestidos de un glamour incuestionable. Un almuerzo en esta ciudad puede basarse en una mariscada monumental de bogavantes y ostras en el acogedor horno y bistró francés Balthazar, o en una hamburguesa de diseño en miniatura servida en el restaurante Pop Burger, de un lujoso estilo retro.

Con sus prestigiosos restaurantes, sus boutiques extremadamente chic y su público internacional a la última, Nueva York, la Gran Manzana, ha definido y define continuamente las últimas tendencias del país.

Patrice Farameh

RESTAURANTS & CAFÉS

Ago Restaurant

377 Greenwich Street at North Moore Street
New York, NY 10013
TriBeCa
Phone: +1 / 212 / 9 25 37 97
www.agorestaurant.com

Opening hours: Sun–Thu 7 am to 11 pm, Fri–Sat 7 am to midnight
Prices: $$$$
Cuisine: Italian
Subway: 1 at Franklin Street
Map: No. 1

Lydia Hearst's Special Tip
A vast assortment of delectable foods and a friendly wait staff in an impressive space.

Joining existing outposts in LA, Vegas, and South Beach, Robert De Niro's Ago occupies a prized place in TriBeCa's Greenwich Hotel—also owned by De Niro. The menu offers well-executed "greatest hits" of modern Italian cuisine including thin pizzas, a 22-ounce steak and the acclaimed linguine with clams.

Zu den bereits existierenden Lokalen in LA, Vegas und South Beach kommt nun noch ein weiteres hinzu: Robert De Niros Ago ist in TriBeCas Greenwich Hotel – das ebenfalls De Niro gehört – bestens gelegen. Die Karte bietet die „Greatest Hits" der modernen italienischen Küche in bester Manier, darunter dünne Pizzen, ein 600-Gramm-Steak und die hoch gelobten Linguine mit Muscheln.

A l'instar des restaurants déjà ouverts à Los Angeles, Las Vegas et South Beach, le restaurant Ago, dont le propriétaire est Robert De Niro, tient une place très prisée dans le Greenwich Hôtel – appartenant lui aussi à De Niro. Le menu offre des « incontournables » de la cuisine italienne moderne comme les pizzas à pâte fine, le steak de 600 grammes et les très appréciés linguines aux palourdes.

El restaurante Ago de Robert De Niro, que se suma a las filiales que la cadena ya poseía en Los Ángeles, Las Vegas y South Beach, ocupa un lugar privilegiado dentro del Greenwich Hotel de TriBeCa –del cual De Niro también es propietario. El menú ofrece "grandes éxitos" de la cocina italiana bien elaborados e incluye pizzas de masa fina, un bistec de ternera de 600 gramos y los célebres linguine con almejas.

Balthazar

80 Spring Street at Crosby Street
New York, NY 10012
SoHo
Phone: +1 / 212 / 9 65 14 14
www.balthazarny.com

Opening hours: Mon–Fri 7:30 am to 11:30 am, noon to 5 pm, Raw Bar 5 pm to 6 pm, 6 pm to 12:30 am, Fri 1:30 am; Sat 8 am to 10 am, Raw Bar 4 pm to 6 pm, 6 pm to 1:30 am; Sun 8 am to 10 am, Raw Bar 4 pm to 5:30 pm, 5:30 pm to 12:30 am; Weekend Brunch 10 am to 4 pm
Prices: $$$
Cuisine: French
Subway: N, R, W at Prince Street; 6 at Spring Street; B, D, F, V at Broadway-Lafayette Street
Map: No. 2

Lydia Hearst's Special Tip
Very popular with the entertainment industry, the atmosphere is perfectly Parisian and always hopping.

Keith McNally's Paris via Spring Street bistro brings together the best of both worlds. Classic French touches like the zinc bar and softly lit wall sconces provide the backdrop to an ambient energy level that is decidedly more Manhattan than Marais. The menu is classic French, the baked goods outstanding.

Das Bistro Keith McNallys führt uns über die Spring Street nach Paris und verbindet dabei das Beste der beiden Welten: Klassische französische Einflüsse wie die Zink-Bar und der Wandleuchter mit gedämmtem Licht bilden die Kulisse für ein Ambiente voller Energie, das eindeutig eher Manhattan als Marais ist. Die Karte ist klassisch französisch, die Backwaren herausragend gut.

Le bistrot style parisien de Keith McNally sur Spring Street mélange le meilleur des deux pays. La touche française avec son zinc et la douce lumière offre une ambiance pleine de vie qui fait plus Manhattan que Marais. Le menu est typiquement français et les pâtisseries sont délicieuses.

El bistró de Keith McNally nos traslada a París a través de la calle Spring Street de Nueva York hasta un local que reúne lo mejor de ambos mundos. Los toques franceses clásicos como el bar de cinc y los apliques de luz tenue proporcionan un ambiente cargado de energía que es decididamente más Manhattan que Marais. El menú ofrece platos franceses clásicos y la repostería es extraordinaria.

Blue Water Grill

31 Union Square West at 16th Street
New York, NY 10003
Phone: +1 / 212 / 6 75 95 00
www.brguestrestaurants.com

Opening hours: Mon–Wed 11:30 am to 11 pm, Thu 11:30 am to midnight, Fri–Sat 11:30 am
to 12:30 am, Sun 10:30 am to 11 pm
Prices: $$$
Cuisine: American Nouveau, seafood
Subway: N, R, Q, W, 4, 5, 6, L at Union Square
Map: No. 3

Lydia Hearst's Special Tip
With excellent food and service, this a wonderful place to go for weekend brunch and to people watch.

Located in an opulent marble structure that was a bank in its previous life, this bi-level Union Square
establishment serves amazing seafood in innovative ways. Choose from lobster salad sliders and
mouthwatering sushi creations and be sure to take advantage of the seasonal outdoor terrace if
you can.

Dieses zweistöckige Restaurant in einem luxuriösen Marmorgebäude am Union Square, das einst
eine Bank beherbergte, bietet unglaublich guten und innovativ zubereiteten Fisch und Meeresfrüchte.
Es gibt eine Auswahl zwischen Hummersalat und Sushi-Kreationen, bei denen einem das Wasser im
Munde zusammen läuft. Wenn möglich, sollte man unbedingt auf der während der Saison geöffneten
Terrasse Platz nehmen.

Dans un bâtiment en marbre assez opulent qui abrita autrefois une banque, cet établissement de
Union Square bâti sur deux étages, sert des plats de fruits de mer vraiment innovants. À vous de choi-
sir entre les brioches à la salade de homard et les appétissantes créations de sushi. Ne manquez pas
de réserver votre place en terrasse quand le temps est de la partie.

Este restaurante está ubicado en un opulento edificio de mármol de dos pisos en la plaza Union Square.
En el local que antiguamente fuera un banco, hoy se sirve marisco de la mejor calidad preparado de
formas innovadoras. Elija entre los panecillos rellenos de ensalada de bogavante y los apetitosos boca-
dos de sushi. La terraza, que abre por temporadas, también es digna de mención.

RESTAURANTS & CAFÉS . Blue Water Grill   27

Café Sabarsky

1048 5th Avenue at 86th Street
New York, NY 10028
Upper East Side
Phone: +1 / 212 / 2 88 06 65
www.neuegalerie.org

Opening hours: Mon 9 am to 6 pm, Tue closed, Wed 9 am to 6 pm, Thu–Sun 9 am to 9 pm
Prices: $$$
Cuisine: German, Austrian
Subway: 4, 5, 6 at 86th Street
Map: No. 4

Located at the Neue Galerie museum, this sophisticated café offers one of the most civilized dining experiences around. Looking out onto Fifth Avenue and Central Park, Viennese pastries and silver tea services transport patrons to turn-of-the-century Europe. Perfect for a light lunch or afternoon tea.

Dieses gehobene Café im Neue Galerie Museum bietet eines der kultiviertesten Dinner-Erlebnisse, die man in der Umgebung finden kann. Mit Blick auf die Fifth Avenue und den Central Park, dem Wiener Feingebäck und den silbernen Teeservices fühlen sich die Gäste wie zu Beginn des letzten Jahrhunderts in Europa. Wunderbar geeignet für ein leichtes Mittagessen oder den Nachmittagstee.

Situé dans le musée Neue Galerie, ce café sophistiqué propose une des expériences culinaires des plus raffinées de la ville. Une vue sur la Fifth Avenue et Central Park, les viennoiseries et les services à thé en argent transportent la clientèle dans l'Europe du début du XXème siècle. Parfait pour un déjeuner léger ou un thé dans l'après midi.

El sofisticado café dentro del museo de la Neue Galerie ofrece una de las proposiciones gastronómicas más refinadas de la zona. Con su repostería vienesa y sus juegos de té plateados, este local con vistas a la Fifth Avenue y a Central Park hace que uno se sienta transportado a la Europa del cambio de siglo. El lugar idóneo para un almuerzo ligero o un té al caer la tarde.

Katz's Delicatessen

205 East Houston Street at Ludlow Street
New York, NY 10002
Lower East Side
Phone: +1 / 212 / 2 54 22 46
www.katzdeli.com

Opening hours: Mon–Tue 8 am to 9:45 pm, Wed–Thu 8 am to 10:45 pm, Fri–Sat 8 am to 2:45 am, Sun 8 am to 10:45 pm
Prices: $$
Cuisine: American traditional, Eastern European
Subway: F, V at Lower East Side-2nd Avenue
Map: No. 5

Russell James' Special Tip
This Jewish deli recalls an era when no one cared about waistlines. A corned beef sandwich could feed two.

A New York institution, this iconic old-school delicatessen starred in the most memorable scene of *When Harry Met Sally*. Their pièce de résistance is the pastrami on rye. The bustling cafeteria-style dining room is among the last of its kind and calls to mind a New York culture that has all but vanished.

Eine Institution New Yorks. In diesem Kultrestaurant mit Delikatessen von der alten Schule, wurde einst die unvergessliche Szene von *Harry und Sally* gedreht. Die Spezialität des Hauses ist hier Pastrami auf Roggenbrot. Der belebte Speiseraum im Cafeteria-Stil ist einer der letzten seiner Art und erinnert an eine New York-Kultur, die alles andere als verschwunden ist.

Une institution New-yorkaise. Cette icône de la charcuterie à l'ancienne est aussi célèbre pour la fameuse scène de *Quand Harry rencontre Sally*. Leur pièce de résistance est le bœuf fumé sur pain de seigle. La salle à manger de style cafétéria est l'une des dernières du genre et rappelle une culture new-yorkaise qui est toujours aussi vivante.

Este icónico restaurante gourmet de la vieja escuela, donde se filmó la más memorable escena de la película *Harry y Sally*, es toda una institución en Nueva York. El sándwich de pastrami es el protagonista absoluto de la carta. El bullicioso comedor con aires de cafetería es uno de los últimos de su especie y trae a la memoria una cara de Nueva York que aún no ha desaparecido del todo.

Keens Steakhouse

72 West 36th Street
New York, NY 10018
Midtown West
Phone: +1 / 212 / 9 47 36 36
www.keens.com

Opening hours: Mon–Fri 11:45 am to 10:30 pm, Sat 5 pm to 10:30 pm, Sun 5 pm to 9 pm
Prices: $$$$
Cuisine: Steakhouse
Subway: N, R, Q, W, B, D, F, V to 34th Street
Map: No. 6

Since 1885, this midtown chophouse has been a haven from nearby Herald Square. They serve what is reputed to be one of the city's best martinis and a menu that recalls Golden Age New York with oysters Rockefeller, classic shrimp cocktail and various aged cuts including a "legendary" mutton chop.

Seit 1885 ist dieses zentral gelegene Steakhaus der Zufluchtsort für Gäste vom nahe gelegenen Herald Square. Hier wird angeblich einer der besten Martinis der Stadt ausgeschenkt und ein Menü serviert, das mit Austern à la Rockefeller, klassischen Schrimp-Cocktails und verschiedenen gut abgehangenen Fleischstücken, darunter das legendäre Lammkotelett, an New Yorks Goldene Zeiten erinnert.

Depuis 1885, ce grill du centre ville est un vrai sanctuaire au milieu de la jungle d'Herald Square. Il a la réputation de servir les meilleurs Martinis de la ville et un menu qui rappelle l'âge d'or de New York avec des huîtres Rockefeller, le classique cocktail de crevettes et diverses pièces de viande comme sa légendaire cote de mouton.

Desde 1885, este céntrico restaurante especializado en carnes constituye un refugio privilegiado dentro de la zona del Herald Square. Los martinis que aquí se sirven están considerados unos de los mejores de la ciudad y su carta rememora los años dorados de Nueva York con platos como las ostras Rockefeller, el clásico cóctel de gambas y una gran variedad de carnes añejas, entre las que se incluyen también las legendarias chuletas de cordero.

Miss Keens

La Esquina

114 Kenmare Street at Lafayette Street
New York, NY 10012
Little Italy
Phone: +1 / 646 / 6 13 71 00
www.esquinanyc.com

Opening hours: Taqueria: Mon–Fri 8 am to 11:30 am and noon to 2 am daily; Delivery Mon–Fri noon to 11 pm, Sat–Sun noon to 10 pm; Café: noon to midnight daily, Brunch Sat–Sun 11 am to 4 pm; Brasserie & Tequila Bar: 6 pm to 2 am daily
Prices: $$$
Cuisine: Latin American
Subway: 6 at Spring Street
Map: No. 7

Lydia Hearst's Special Tip
While the entrance is hard to find, this darkly seductive dining room is one of the top Mexican restaurants.

What appears to be a shabby chic taco stand at first glance gives way to a cavernous lower level—accessed by a "hidden" passage that goes through the kitchen. Once in, the space is sexy and candlelit corners encourage canoodling. Menu offers small plates as well as regular courses.

Was auf den ersten Blick wie eine schäbig-schicke Taco-Bude erscheint, entpuppt sich auf der unteren Etage, zu der man durch einen „Geheimgang" durch die Küche gelangt, als eine Grotte, deren sexy Ambiente und mit Kerzen beleuchtete Ecken zu romantischen Stunden einladen. Die Karte bietet kleine Snacks und konventionelle Gerichte.

Ce qui ressemble à première vue à un stand à tacos miteux, fait place à un sous-soul gigantesque accessible par un passage secret à travers la cuisine. Une fois à l'intérieur, la salle et la lumière des chandelles invitent à un dîner romantique. Au menu : petits plats et plats plus classiques.

Lo que a primera vista parece un puesto de venta de tacos mejicanos al estilo chic desarrapado, revela una planta baja cavernosa a la que uno accede pasando a través de un corredor "escondido" en la cocina. Su interior ampara un ambiente íntimo, con rincones a la luz de las velas que exhalan romanticismo. El menú incluye pequeños tentempiés y platos convencionales.

Matsugen

241 Church Street at Leonard Street
New York, NY 10013
TriBeCa
Phone: +1 / 212 / 9 25 02 02
www.jean-georges.com

Opening hours: Mon–Sun noon to 3 pm, Mon–Thu 5:30 pm to 1 am, Fri–Sat 5:30 pm to 2 am,
Sun 5:30 pm to 1 am
Prices: $$$$
Cuisine: Japanese, Sushi
Subway: 1 at Franklin Street
Map: No. 8

Jean-Georges Vongerichten brings the traditional Japanese art of making soba noodles to TriBeCa in
this sleek Thomas Juul-Hansen-designed restaurant. Sushiphiles, look elsewhere. At Matsugen, the
focus is on Japanese home cooking including soup-based dishes and *shabu shabu*: reinvented comfort
food, Nipponese style.

Jean-Georges Vongerichten bringt in diesem gepflegten, von Thomas Juul-Hansen designten Restaurant
die traditionelle japanische Kunst der Zubereitung von Soba-Nudeln nach TriBeCa. Sushi-Liebhaber
haben hier eher nichts zu suchen: Im Matsugen steht die japanische Hausmannskost mit ihren auf
Suppen basierenden Gerichten und *Shabu Shabu* im Mittelpunkt. Die Hausmannskost im Nippon-Style
wird hier neu definiert.

Jean-Georges Vongerichten amène l'art traditionnel des nouilles soba à TriBeCa avec ce restaurant
élégant conçu par le designer Thomas Juul-Hansen. Les « sushiphiles » doivent chercher ailleurs. Au
Matsugen, l'honneur est à la cuisine japonaise maison avec ses plats à base de soupes et le *shabu
shabu*: cuisine facile, réinventée au style japonais.

Con este elegante restaurante de interiores diseñados por Thomas Juul-Hansen, Jean-Georges Vongerichten ha llevado a TriBeCa el arte tradicional japonés de elaborar los finos fideos soba de harina
de alforfón. Los meros amantes del sushi no encontrarán sus platos favoritos aquí. En el Matsugen la
cocina se centra en platos japoneses caseros, sopas y *shabu-shabu*, la reinvención de una comida con
sabor de hogar al más puro estilo nipón.

Merkato 55

55 Gansevoort Street
New York, NY 10014
Meatpacking District
Phone: +1 / 212 / 2 55 85 55
www.merkato55nyc.com

Opening hours: Mon–Fri 5:30 pm to midnight, Sat–Sun 11:30 am to 3 pm and 5:30 pm to midnight
Prices: $$$
Cuisine: African, Moroccan
Subway: A, C, E, L at 14th Street
Map: No. 9

Merkato 55 is the culinary equivalent of a tour of Africa, with influences ranging from the Mediterranean to sub-Saharan. Its three levels are decked out in warm chocolatey tones, setting the scene for a succession of spice-infused small and large plates. Desserts come highly recommended.

Die Küche des Merkato 55 ist voller Einflüsse, die vom Mittelmeer bis hin zur Subsahara reichen und in kulinarischer Hinsicht einer Afrikareise gleichzustellen. Die drei Etagen sind in warmen, schokofarbenen Tönen eingerichtet und bilden die passende Kulisse, um die perfekt gewürzten Gerichte für den kleinen und den großen Hunger zu genießen. Die Desserts sind wärmstens zu empfehlen.

Merkato 55, avec sa cuisine qui tire sa diversité d'influences allant de la Méditerranée aux pays du Sud du Sahara, est l'équivalent d'un voyage culinaire en l'Afrique. Le parquet des trois étages du restaurant ont des tons chocolatés, créant ainsi la scène parfaite pour une succession de petits et grands plats aux accords épicés. Nous vous recommandons vivement les desserts.

El restaurante Merkato 55 es el equivalente culinario a un viaje por África; su cocina está llena de influencias que van desde el mediterráneo hasta el África subsahariana. Los tres pisos que lo componen están decorados en cálidos tonos chocolate y configuran el ambiente idóneo donde disfrutar de una sucesión de pequeños y grandes platos condimentados a la perfección. Se recomiendan especialmente los postres.

Nobu 57

40 West 57th Street
New York, NY 10019
Midtown West
Phone: +1 / 212 / 7 57 30 00
www.noburestaurants.com

Opening hours: Mon–Fri 11:45 am to 2:15 pm and 5 pm to noon, Sat 5 pm to midnight, Sun 5 pm to 11 pm
Prices: $$$
Cuisine: New style Japanese
Subway: F at 57th Street
Map: No. 10

Nobu Matsuhisa's famous black cod with miso comes to Midtown. The interior is a good match for the hectic pace of the neighborhood, with a bar scene comprised of single professionals that outpaces the noise level and energy of the TriBeCa location. The chocolate cake and green tea ice cream *bentō* box is not to be missed.

Nobu Matsuhisas berühmten schwarzen Kabeljau mit Miso gibt es jetzt auch in Midtown. Das Interior dieses Lokals passt sehr gut zum hektischen Treiben dieses Viertels. An der Bar sitzen alleinstehende Geschäftsleute und sowohl Geräuschpegel als auch die hier verspürte Energie übertreffen das Restaurant in TriBeCa. Den Schokoladenkuchen und die Eiscreme aus grünem Tee, serviert in einer *Bentō*-Box, muss man unbedingt probiert haben!

La célèbre morue noire au miso de Nobu Matsuhisa arrive au centre ville. L'intérieur se marie parfaitement au rythme frénétique du voisinage. Avec une clientèle de professionnels célibataires plus bruyante et énergétique que le quartier vibrant de TriBeCa. Le gateau au chocolat et la glace au thé vert dans sa boite *bentō* doivent être à tout prix être gouté.

En este local de la zona de Midtown se puede degustar el famoso bacalao negro con miso de Nobu Matsuhisa. Su interior armoniza con el frenético ritmo de vida del barrio, donde los bares poblados de jóvenes ejecutivos solteros crean un nivel de ruido y una energía superiores a los de TriBeCa. Obligado probar la caja *bentō* con tarta de chocolate y helado de té verde.

Peasant

194 Elizabeth Street
New York, NY 10012
NoLIta
Phone: +1 / 212 / 9 65 95 11
www.peasantnyc.com

Opening hours: Mon closed, Tue–Sat 6 pm to 11 pm, Sun 6 pm to 11 pm
Prices: $$$
Cuisine: Italian
Subway: 6 at Spring Street; N, R at Prince Street
Map: No. 11

Upstairs/downstairs rustic Italian in Nolita. The street level is home to the main dining room while the romantic, arch-ceilinged wine cellar has its own entrance and offers a mix of shareable Tuscan plates and entrees cooked over an open fire. The low lighting and brick walls further add to the atmosphere.

Ein rustikaler Italiener auf zwei Etagen in Nolita. In der oberen Ebene befindet sich auf Straßenhöhe der Hauptspeiseraum, während der romantische Gewölbe-Weinkeller mit eigenem Eingang eine Mischung aus toskanischen Vorspeisen und Hauptgerichten bietet, die auf offenem Feuer zubereitet werden. Das gedämmte Licht und die Backsteinmauern runden die angenehme Atmosphäre ab.

Italien rustique sur deux étages à Nolita. Le rez de chaussée accueille la grande salle de restaurant tandis que la romantique cave à vin voutée possède sa propre entrée et propose diverses assiettes toscanes à partager et des entrées préparées sur feu ouvert. La lumière tamisée et les murs de brique ajoutent à l'atmosphère.

Restaurante italiano rústico de dos plantas en Nolita. La primera planta alberga el comedor principal y la romántica bodega de techos de bóveda con entrada propia ofrece una mezcla de entrantes y platos toscanos para compartir elaborados a lumbre. La iluminación tenue y las murallas de ladrillo contribuyen a redondear la atmósfera de este local.

Philippe Chow

33 East 60th Street
New York, NY 10022
Upper East Side
Phone: +1 / 212 / 6 44 88 85
www.philippechow.com

Opening hours: Mon–Sat noon to 4 pm and 6 pm to midnight, Sun 3 pm to midnight
Prices: $$$$
Cuisine: Chinese
Subway: N, R, W at 5th Avenue
Map: No. 12

Mr. Chow's veteran chef Philippe Chow (no relation between the two Chows) ventured out on his own with this swanky, sexy addition to the haute Chinese culinary scene. With three intimate dining areas, this is the perfect place for a special first date. The Peking duck is recommended and prepared tableside.

Philippe Chow, ehemals Chefkoch im Mr. Chow (die beiden Chows sind nicht miteinander verwandt), hat einiges gewagt, als er der chinesischen Haute Cuisine seine eigene elegante, sexy Note hinzufügte. Mit seinen drei intimen Speiseräumen ist dies der perfekte Ort für ein erstes Date. Zu empfehlen ist die Pekingente, die am Tisch zubereitet wird.

Le chef expérimenté de Mr. Chow's, Philippe Chow (aucun lien entre les deux Chow) est parti a l'aventure en apportant une touche sexy et huppée dans le milieu de la haute cuisine Chinoise. Avec ses trois salles, c'est l'endroit parfait pour un premier rendez vous. Le canard laqué est conseillé et il est préparé à table.

Philippe Chow adquirió largos años de experiencia como cocinero en el restaurante Mr. Chow (sin relación familiar) e inició su carrera en solitario con este restaurante, que constituye un complemento elegante y sexy dentro de la esfera gastronómica de la alta cocina china. Los tres comedores de ambiente íntimo constituyen el entorno perfecto para una primera cita especial. Se recomienda el pato Pekín preparado junto a la mesa.

Pop Burger

58–60 9th Avenue
New York, NY 10011
Meatpacking District
Phone: +1 / 212 / 4 14 86 86
www.popburger.com

Opening hours: Mon–Wed 11 am to 2 am, Thu–Sat 11 am to 5 am, Sun 11 am to 2 am
Prices: $$
Cuisine: Hamburgers, hot dogs
Subway: A, C, E, L at 14th Street
Map: No. 13

Lydia Hearst's Special Tip
These trendy cafés are popping up all over town! A great place to grab a bite with friends, dance among celebrities, or get a burger and fries to go.

A grown-up place for guilty-pleasure favorites like burgers, fries and shakes. Pop Burger proves that chic fast food is not an oxymoron. The Meatpacking joint manages to balance sexy ambient lighting with relaxed décor and an informal scene. At night, it transforms into a lounge, with drinks and DJs late into the night.

Ein Lokal für Erwachsene, in dem verbotene Lieblingsgelüste nach Burgern, Pommes und Milchshakes befriedigt werden. Pop Burger ist der Beweis dafür, dass schickes Fastfood kein Widerspruch in sich ist. Das Lokal im Meatpacking District schafft es, ein Gleichgewicht zwischen sexy Beleuchtung, entspanntem Dekor und informellem Ambiente zu schaffen. Nachts verwandelt es sich in eine Lounge, in der Drinks angeboten werden und DJs bis spät in die Nacht auflegen.

Un endroit pour les adultes, avec des petits plaisirs culinaires comme burgers, frites et milk-shakes. Pop Burger prouve que le fast-food et le chic ne sont pas incompatibles. Cet établissement du Meatpacking arrive à lier une touche romantique à un décor relax dans une ambiance plutôt informelle. Le soir Pop Burger se transforme en lounge, avec boissons et DJ's jusqu'au bout de la nuit.

Un lugar de clientela adulta para deleitarse con algunos de los placeres prohibidos de la cocina americana: hamburguesas, patatas fritas y batidos. Este restaurante demuestra que lo chic y la comida rápida no tienen porqué estar reñidos. Esta filial del distrito de Meatpacking consigue armonizar una sugerente iluminación y una decoración interior relajada con un ambiente informal. Durante la noche se convierte en un bar-lounge de copas con pinchadiscos abierto hasta muy tarde.

hot burgers, cool and frosty soda

creamy shakes
mouth watering
pop hot burgers
warm buns, creamy
firm fries, sizzling
cool and frosty soda,
sizzling steaks, firm
creamy shakes, luscious
frosty soda, hot burgers
pop, cool and frosty soda
warm buns, pop, firm fries,
luscious mouth watering warm buns
firm fries, creamy shakes, hot burgers

Spice Market

403 West 13th Street
New York, NY 10014
Meatpacking District
Phone: +1 / 212 / 6 75 23 22
www.spicemarketnewyork.com

Opening hours: Mon–Wed noon to 4 pm and 5:30 pm to midnight, Thu–Sat noon to 4 pm and 5:30 pm to 1 am, Sun noon to 4 pm and 5:30 pm to midnight
Prices: $$$
Cuisine: Southeast Asian, Thai
Subway: A, C, E, L at 14th Street
Map: No. 14

Foodies and fête-seekers venture to the Meatpacking District for celebuchef Jean-Georges Vongerichten's two-story Southeast Asian fantasy palace. Both the interior design and the menu are seamless executions of sophisticated fun: palm trees, silk lanterns, lychee martinis and reinvented Thai classics.

Gourmets und Gäste auf der Suche nach etwas Festlichkeit treffen sich im Meatpacking District im zweistöckigen südostasiatischen Fantasietempel des berühmten Chefkochs Jean-Georges Vongerichten. Die Inneneinrichtung und die Karte sind Ausdruck eleganter Verspieltheit: Palmen, Seidenlaternen, Lychee-Martinis und wiederentdeckte Thai-Klassiker.

Amateurs de bonne cuisine et fêtards en veine de réjouissances se rencontrent dans le Meatpacking District, dans le palais des fantaisies sur deux étages du restaurant du célèbre chef Jean-Georges Vongerichten. Le menu autant que le décor traduisent à merveille cet univers empreint d'élégante imagination : avec palmiers, lanternes de soie, martinis au lychee et classiques de la cuisine Thaï réinventés.

Los amantes de la buena mesa y aquellos en busca de diversión acuden al distrito de Meatpacking para aventurarse en el restaurante Spice Market del célebre chef Jean-Georges Vongerichten. Las dos plantas de este lugar lleno de fantasía recrean el sureste asiático. Su decoración interior y su carta son toda una muestra de diversión sofisticada: palmeras, lamparillas de seda, martinis con lichi y clásicos de la cocina tailandesa reinventados.

The Mercer Kitchen

99 Spring Street at Mercer Street
New York, NY 10012
SoHo
Phone: +1 / 212 / 9 66 54 54
www.mercerhotel.com

Opening hours: Mon–Thu 7 am to 3 pm and 6 pm to midnight, Fri 7 am to 3 pm and 5:30 pm
to 1 am, Sat 7 am to 4 pm and 5:30 pm to 1 am, Sun 7 am to 4 pm and 5:30 pm to 11 am
Prices: $$$
Cuisine: American Nouveau, Southeast Asian, French
Nearby Subway Stops: N, R, W at Prince Street
Map: No. 15

Lydia Hearst's Special Tip
*Located in the heart of SoHo, this place has a great atmosphere. As you are walking through, you may
just see celebrity guests!*

French designer Christian Liaigre's clean-lined subterranean dining room is a SoHo fixture. Since 1998,
the Mercer has been the setting for some of the fashion world's most important meetings. The upstairs
bar area is great for a tête-à-tête over drinks or a quick bite from Jean-Georges' modern American
menu.

Der vom französischen Designer Christian Liaigre entworfene unterirdische Diningroom mit den klaren
Linien gehört mittlerweile zum Inventar von SoHo. Seit 1998 fanden im Mercer einige der wichtigsten
Meetings der Modewelt statt. Die Bar auf der oberen Etage eignet sich hervorragend für ein Tête-à-tête
bei einem Drink oder einem kleinen Snack aus der modernen amerikanischen Karte von Jean-Georges.

La salle de restaurant en sous sol designée par le français Christian Liaigre est devenu un incontour-
nable de SoHo. Depuis 1998, The Mercer à été le théâtre des rendez-vous les plus importants dans le
domaine de la mode mondiale. Le bar à l'étage est parfait pour quelques verres en tête-à-tête ou pour
grignoter un petit plat du menu américain moderne de Jean Georges.

Este comedor subterráneo de marcada decoración fue diseñado por Christian Liaigre y es ya todo un
distintivo del barrio del SoHo. Desde 1998 el restaurante Mercer ha sido el escenario de algunas de
las reuniones más importantes del mundo de la moda. El bar en el piso de arriba es idóneo para pasar
una íntima velada de charla y copas, o para probar alguno de los tentempiés del menú americano
moderno de Jean-Georges.

CLUBS, LOUNGES & BARS

230 Fifth

230 5th Avenue
New York, NY 10001
Flatiron
Phone: +1 / 212 / 7 25 43 00
www.230-fifth.com

Opening hours: Mon–Sun 4 pm to 4 am
Prices: $$$
Subway: N, R, W at 28th Street
Map: No. 16

This 22,000-square-foot rooftop lounge in the Flatiron neighborhood offers its patrons amazing views. Palm trees and fountains exude 1940s cool and the result is an oasis of Los Angeles-style glamour amidst the skyscrapers. The outdoor area is open seasonally but the Penthouse Lounge is open all year long.

Diese ca. 2000m² große Dachlounge in der Nähe vom Flatiron-Building bietet seinen Gästen eine unglaubliche Aussicht. Palmen und Brunnen strahlen eine coole Atmosphäre der 40er Jahre aus, und das Ergebnis ist eine Glamour-Oase im Los Angeles-Stil inmitten der Hochhäuser. Der Garten kann nur in der Sommersaison besucht werden, die Penthouse Lounge hingegen ist das ganze Jahr über geöffnet.

Ce salon de 2,000m² sur les toits dans le quartier du Flatiron offre des vues magnifiques à ses clients. Palmiers et fontaines rappellent les années 40 et le résultat est un oasis de glamour à la Los Angeles parmi les gratte-ciels. L'espace extérieur est ouvert de manière saisonnière, mais le salon Penthouse est lui ouvert tout l'année.

Este lounge-bar del barrio de Flatiron, situado en una azotea de cerca de 2.000 metros cuadrados, ofrece a sus visitantes unas vistas maravillosas. Sus palmeras y fuentes transmiten el ambiente relajado y sofisticado de los años 40; el resultado es un oasis al estilo glamoroso de Los Ángeles en medio de los rascacielos de Nueva York. La terraza al aire libre abre sólo por temporadas, pero el lujoso lounge del ático atiende a sus clientes durante todo el año.

APT

419 West 13th Street
New York, NY 10014
Meatpacking District
Phone: +1 / 212 / 4 14 42 45
www.aptnyc.com

Opening hours: Mon–Sun 7 pm to 4 am
Prices: $$$
Subway: A, C, E, L at 14th Street
Map: No. 17

Located in a nondescript former butcher shop on far west 13th Street, APT pioneered the "secret bar" trend in New York nightlife. The tiny downstairs has played host to big name DJs while the upstairs is designed to look like the bourgeois pied-à-terre of a mysterious real-life occupant.

Die Bar APT, die sich in einer nicht weiter interessanten ehemaligen Fleischerei in der West 13th Street befindet, ist eine der ersten, die das Phänomen der „geheimen" Bars in New Yorks Nachtleben gebracht hat. In dem kleinen untergeschossigen Raum haben schon viele berühmte DJs aufgelegt, während das Obergeschoss eher die bürgerliche Bleibe einer geheimnisvollen Person zu sein scheint.

Situé dans les murs d'une ancienne boucherie à l'Ouest de la 13ème rue, APT à été le pionnier en ce qui concerne les « bars cachés » de la nuit new-yorkaise. La petite salle en bas a déjà accueilli beaucoup de DJ de renom tandis que l'étage est emménagé comme le pied-à-terre bourgeois d'un vrai locataire.

Ubicado en una antigua y anodina carnicería al oeste de la calle 13th Street, el bar APT fue unos de los primeros locales que contribuyeron a crear la moda de los "bares secretos" en la vida nocturna de Nueva York. En la minúscula planta baja se dan cita afamados pinchadiscos y la planta superior está diseñada para asemejarse a un apartamento aburguesado donde habita un misterioso personaje de la vida real.

BIJOUX

57 Gansevoort Street
New York, NY 10014
Meatpacking District
Phone: +1 / 12 / 2 55 85 55
www.bijouxlounge.com

Opening hours: Mon–Sun 11 pm to 4 am
Prices: $$$
Subway: A, C, E, L at 14th Street
Map: No. 18

This jewel-box sized boîte is tucked beneath the main dining room of Merkato 55. Décor can be described as sexy-baroque-fairy tale with a gigantic crystal chandelier and a foggy well in the room's center. The low-lit lounge is a current favorite among the socials and celebs who charm their way past the hidden door.

Dieser Nachtclub ist fast so winzig wie ein Schmuckkästchen und liegt versteckt unter dem Hauptspeiseraum des Merkato 55. Die Einrichtung mit dem großen kristallenen Kronleuchter und dem rauchenden Brunnen in der Mitte des Raumes könnte als attraktive Mischung aus barockem und märchenhaftem Stil beschrieben werden. Diese schummrige Lounge ist derzeit unter den Partygängern und Berühmtheiten, die sich durch die versteckte Tür stehlen, besonders beliebt.

Cette boite de la taille d'un écrin à bijoux est située sous la salle principale du restaurant Merkato 55. Le décor peut être décrit comme un conte de fée sexy et baroque avec un chandelier géant en cristal et un puits aux songes au milieu de la pièce. Le salon tamisé est un endroit prisé des célébrités qui apparaissent comme par enchantement par la porte secrète.

Este pequeño bar nocturno, casi del tamaño de un joyero, se encuentra bajo el comedor del Merkato 55. Su diseño interior puede describirse como una atractiva mezcla entre barroco y cuento de hadas, y se caracteriza por una gran lámpara de araña y un nebuloso pozo situados en el centro de la sala. Bajo la tenue iluminación se dan cita estrellas y famosos que, con su encanto, consiguen que se les abra la puerta escondida al BIJOUX.

No Smoking

Cellar Bar

40 West 40th Street
New York, NY 10018
Midtown West
Phone: +1 / 212 / 8 69 01 00
www.bryantparkhotel.com

Opening hours: Mon–Thu 5 pm to 2 am, Fri 5 pm to 4 am, Sat 10 pm to 4 am, Sun closed
Prices: $$$
Subway: 7 at 5th Avenue-Bryant Park, B, D, F, V at 42nd Street-Bryant Park
Map: No. 19

Russell James' Special Tip
After Fashion Week shows wrap in Bryant Park, stroll across the street to this smart underground lounge.

Located in the Bryant Park Hotel, the cavernous downstairs area calls to mind a seriously well-appointed medieval dungeon. Vaulted ceilings and imposing chandeliers lend the room a gothic charm while the DJs and mixologist-approved cocktail menu are as 21st century as it gets. Prime time is after work.

Die Cellar Bar befindet sich im Bryant Park Hotel. Der höhlenartige Raum im Untergeschoss erinnert an ein wirklich gut ausgestattetes mittelalterliches Burgverlies. Die gewölbte Decke und die beeindruckenden Kerzenleuchter verleihen dem Raum einen gotischen Charme, wohingegen die DJs und die Cocktailkarte, die jeder Barkeeper zu loben weiß, so sehr aus dem 21. Jahrhundert stammen, wie dies nur geht. Am meisten besucht ist die Bar beim After Work.

A l'intérieur du Bryant Park Hotel, le sous-sol de ce bar possède des aspects de donjon médiéval. Les voûtes et les chandeliers imposants apportent un charme gothique à la pièce pendant que DJ et carte des cocktails sont, quant à eux, très 21ème siècle. Le meilleur moment d'en profiter ? Juste après les heures de bureau.

Ubicado en el Bryant Park Hotel, la cavernosa estancia en el piso de abajo recuerda a una mazmorra medieval muy bien decorada. El techo abovedado y las lámparas de araña otorgan un encanto gótico al lugar, pero los pinchadiscos de moda y la carta de cócteles, que recibiría el visto bueno de cualquier barman experimentado, nos devuelven indudablemente al siglo XXI. El local se llena a la hora del cierre de oficinas.

Cielo

18 Little West 12th Street
New York, NY 10014
Meatpacking District
Phone: +1 / 212 / 6 45 57 00
www.cieloclub.com

Opening hours: Mon–Sun 10 pm to 4 am
Prices: $$$
Subway: A, C, E, L at 14th Street
Map: No. 20

Since the days of Giuliani, the death of the New York club scene has been an oft-heard lament. Cielo's arrival in the Meatpacking District, however, made these complaints less convincing than ever. Winner of international awards for its sound system and the caliber of DJs that come through, this is the city's number one spot for electronic music.

Seit Giuliani wird der Tod der New Yorker Club-Szene häufig beklagt. Seit es das Cielo im Meatpacking District gibt, sind diese Beschwerden aber weniger überzeugend denn je. Das international preisge-krönte Sound-System und das Kaliber der DJs, die hier auflegen, haben diesen Club zu New Yorks Nummer Eins der elektronischen Musik gemacht.

Depuis l'époque du maire Giuliani, les lamentations sur la mort de la scène club new-yorkaise sont fré-quentes. Mais l'arrivée du Cielo dans le Meatpacking District a rendu ces plaintes moins convaincantes que jamais. Lauréat de prix internationaux pour sa sono et le calibre des DJ qui y mixent. C'est l'endroit numéro un pour la musique électro.

Desde los días de Giuliani a menudo se han escuchado voces que lamentan la muerte de la vida nocturna de Nueva York, pero desde que Cielo abriera sus puertas en el distrito de Meatpacking, estas quejas han quedado más obsoletas que nunca. Su sistema de sonido, que ha recibido ya varios pre-mios internacionales, y el calibre de los pinchadiscos que pasan por esta sala han convertido el club en el "no va más" de la música electrónica de Nueva York.

Fat Black Pussycat

130 West 3rd Street
New York, NY 10012
West Village
Phone: +1 / 212 / 5 33 47 90
www.thefatblackpussycat.com

Opening hours: Mon–Sun 1 pm to 4 am
Prices: $$
Subway: A, B, C, D, E, F, V at W. 4th Street
Map: No. 21

Located in the space that was once a favorite hangout of Beat writers like Jack Kerouac, this bar stays true to its Greenwich Village roots with wooden booths and photographs of the bygone era. Upstairs is the VIP area, where guests indulge in 10-ounce martinis that come in 31 varieties. Pool, darts and dancing too.

Diese Bar im Greenwich Village, in der sich einst Schriftsteller der Beat-Generation wie Jack Kerouac gerne trafen, bleibt mit ihren langen Holztischen und den Fotos aus vergangenen Zeiten ihren Wurzeln treu. Oben befindet sich die VIP-Area. Hier werden den Gästen 0,3l Martinis in 31 Variationen geboten. Nebenbei kann man noch Billard spielen, darten oder auch tanzen.

Situé dans un des endroits préférés des auteurs de Beat tel que Jack Kerouac, ce bar reste fidèle a ses racines de Greenwich Village avec ses cabines en bois et ses photos d'une époque révolue. La zone VIP se trouve à l'étage où les invités ont le choix entre 31 recettes de martini. On peut aussi y jouer au billard, aux fléchettes ou bien même danser.

Ubicado en un local antiguamente frecuentado por escritores de la generación Beat como Jack Kerouac y decorado con largas mesas de madera y fotografías de antaño, este bar del Greenwich Village se mantiene fiel a las raíces del barrio que lo acoge. En el piso de arriba se encuentra la zona VIP, donde los huéspedes pueden darse el capricho de degustar uno de los martinis de 30 centilitros en 31 varie-dades diferentes. Jugar al billar, a los dardos o bailar también es posible en este local.

Kiss and Fly

409 West 13th Street
New York, NY 10014
Meatpacking District
Phone: +1 / 212 / 2 55 19 33
www.kissandflyclub.com

Opening hours: Mon–Sun 11 pm to 4 am
Prices: $$$
Subway: A, C, E, L at 14th Street
Map: No. 22

The double kisses crowd comes to New York via St. Tropez at this Meatpacking club with a glammed-up Roman bathhouse interior. The Euro jet-set vibe reigns supreme; the club is named after the drop-off area of a French Riviera airport and its clientele seem well accustomed to Cote d'Azur-style cork-popping.

In diesem Club im Meatpacking District, der sich im Glamour-Design eines römischen Badehauses präsentiert, trifft sich ein sich à la St. Tropez mit zwei Küssen begrüßendes Volk. Hier herrscht europäische Jetset-Stimmung. Der Club wurde nach dem Landebereich eines Flughafens an der französischen Riviera benannt, und seine Kundschaft scheint mit dem Korken knallenden Stil der Côte d'Azur bestens vertraut zu sein.

Lieu de rencontre privilégié de la clientèle très tendance de New York dans ce club du Meatpacking district décoré de bains Romains. La vibe de la jet-set européenne règne en maitresse ici. Le club doit son nom à la piste d'atterrissage d'un aéroport de la Côte d'Azur et la clientèle a bien l'habitude du bruit des bouchons de champagne qui sautent.

El público chic de los dos besos al aire que se da cita en este bar del distrito de Meatpacking llega a Nueva York directamente desde Saint-Tropez. En su interior, cuyo diseño recuerda a unos baños romanos redecorados, reina un ambiente de jet-set europea. El bar lleva el nombre de la zona de descanso de un aeropuerto de la Riviera francesa y su clientela parece acostumbrada al sonido de los tapones de champán que se descorchan en la Costa Azul.

Marquee

289 10th Avenue
New York, NY 10001
Chelsea
Phone: +1 / 212 / 64 64 73 02 02
www.marqueeny.com

Opening hours: Mon closed, Tue 10 pm to 4 am, Wed–Sat 10:30 pm to 4 am, Sun closed
Prices: $$$
Subway: C, E at 23rd Street
Map: No. 23

Lydia Hearst's Special Tip
This club has withstood the test of time. Top models and musicians are easy to spot dancing the night away.

This is thee best of the megaclubs that 27th Street has become famous (or infamous) for. Marquee started out as a celebrity magnet, drawing from the same pool of clientele as nearby Bungalow 8. Since then, it has mellowed into less of a scene but remains a favorite among models, promoters and high-rollers.

Dies ist der beste der Megaclubs, für die die 27th Street berühmt (oder eher berüchtigt) ist. Marquee zog zu Anfang die Berühmtheiten an wie ein Magnet und hatte mehr oder weniger dieselbe Kundschaft wie das nahe gelegene Bungalow 8. Auch wenn es hier heute etwas ruhiger zugeht, zählt der Club bei Models, Promotern und betuchten Glücksspielern noch zu den Lieblingsorten.

C'est LE meilleur de tous les méga clubs qui ont rendu 27th Street (tristement ?) célèbre. Véritable appât à célébrités au début, Marquee ciblait plus ou moins la même clientèle que le tout proche Bungalow 8. Même si le club a un peu perdu son statut de rendez-vous de la scène new-yorkaise, il reste toujours un des endroits favoris chez les top-models, promoteurs et les flambeurs.

El mejor de los grandes clubes que han dado fama (o han hecho infame) a la calle 27th Street. El Marquee fue en sus inicios un imán de famosos y compartió clientela con el cercano club Bungalow 8. Desde entonces se ha vuelto un poco más tranquilo, pero sigue siendo un local predilecto por modelos, promotores y grandes derrochadores.

Rose Bar & Jade Bar

2 Lexington Avenue at 21st Street
New York, NY 10010
Gramercy
Phone: +1 / 212 / 9 20 33 00
www.gramercyparkhotel.com

Opening hours: Mon closed, Tue–Sat 5 pm to 4 am, Sun closed
Prices: $$$
Subway: N, R, W, 6 at 23rd Street
Map: No. 24

Russell James' Special Tip
Following shoots, models come for cocktails as dazzling as the lounge's artwork—yes, that's a real Warhol.

The Rose Bar & Jade Bar at the Ian Schrager/Julian Schnabel-redesigned Gramercy Park Hotel are the city's nightlife destinations par excellence. Design-wise, each is heavily imbued with the genius of the hotelier/artist collaboration. The only drawback? A very selective door policy for non-guests.

Die Rose Bar & Jade Bar im von Ian Schrager und Julian Schnabel neu designten Gramercy Park Hotel sind New Yorks Szenetreff par excellence. Was das Design betrifft, sind beide Bars stark von der genialen Zusammenarbeit von Hotelier und Künstler inspiriert worden. Der einzige Haken? Eine streng selektive Türpolitik für alle, die keine Hotelgäste sind.

Le Rose Bar & Jade Bar dans le Gramercy Park Hôtel, rénové par Ian Schrager et Julian Schnabel, sont les destinations par excellence de la vie nocturne à New York. Au niveau design, les deux endroits sont imprégnés du génie de la collaboration entre l'hôtelier et l'artiste. Le seul hic, si l'on n'est pas invité, on rentre difficilement.

Los locales Rose Bar & Jade Bar en el Gramercy Park Hotel, rediseñados por Ian Schrager y Julian Schnabel, constituyen el punto de encuentro por excelencia de la vida nocturna neoyorquina. En cada uno de estos bares se percibe el genio de la colaboración entre el hotelero y el artista. El único inconveniente: una política de admisión muy rigurosa para aquellos que no se hospedan en el hotel.

SHOPS

45rpm

169 Mercer Street
SoHo
Phone: +1 / 917 / 2 37 00 45
New York, NY 10012
www.rby45rpm.com

Opening Hours: Mon–Sat 11 am to 7 pm; Sun 11 am to 6 pm
Products: Clothing, accessories
Subway: N, R at Prince Street
Map: No. 25

Premium jeans turned the Japanese label into a legend. Today the portfolio includes a unisex line, children's fashions, and leather articles. There is constant experimentation with traditional Asian themes, such as sweaters evoking the clothing worn by people in the Himalayas. There are two locations in New York: "R by 45rpm" in Lower Manhattan and "45R" on the Upper East Side.

Premium-Jeans haben das japanische Label zur Legende gemacht. Heute gehören eine Unisex-Linie, Mode für Kinder und Lederwaren zum Portfolio. Immer wieder wird mit traditionellen asiatischen Einflüssen gespielt, so etwa bei Pullovern, die an die Kleidung der Himalaya-Bewohner erinnern. Mit „R by 45rpm" in Lower Manhattan und „45R" an der Upper East Side sind in New York gleich zwei Stores vertreten.

Des jeans de qualité ont fait de cette marque japonaise une légende. La marque propose aujourd'hui une ligne unisexe, de la mode pour enfants et de la maroquinerie dans son catalogue. On retrouve des influences traditionnelles d'Asie comme avec les pullovers qui rappellent ceux portés par les habitants de l'Himalaya. New York abrite 2 magasins avec «R by 45rpm» dans le Manhattan et «45R» dans l'Upper East Side.

Los vaqueros de primera calidad han convertido la marca japonesa en toda una leyenda. Dentro de su gama de productos se pueden encontrar actualmente una línea de prendas unisex, moda para niños y géneros de cuero. Las influencias japonesas tradicionales son una fuente habitual de inspiración para sus creaciones, como por ejemplo los suéteres cuyo diseño recuerda a la ropa de los habitantes del Himalaya. La marca cuenta con dos filiales en Nueva York, "R by 45rpm" en la zona Lower Manhattan y "45R" en el barrio Upper East Side.

ABC Carpet & Home

888 Broadway at 19th Street
New York, NY 10003
Flatiron
Phone: +1 / 212 / 4 73 30 00
www.abchome.com

Opening hours: Mon–Fri 10 am to 8 pm, Sat 10 am to 7 pm, Sun 11 am to 6:30 pm
Products: Antique/vintage furniture, accessories, kitchen/tableware, lighting
Subway: N, R, Q, W, 4, 5, 6, L at Union Square
Map: No. 26

Lydia Hearst's Special Tip
A place where you can shop for antiques or indulge in delicate Michel Cluizel chocolates at their private cafe.

More than 650 pieces offered in this upmarket bazaar of furnishings and finishings for the home are produced sustainable and with a strong regard on social circumstances in the country of production and environmental protection. Beside objets d'art from Congo to India you will find a noteworthy rug selection that includes antiques and hard to find hand-woven pieces from the Orient.

Mehr als ein Drittel aller in diesem Basar der oberen Preisklasse angebotenen Möbelstücke und Zubehöre für das Heim wurden nachhaltig und mit Rücksicht auf die Umwelt und die sozialen Umstände im Produktionsland hergestellt. Abgesehen von Objekten aus dem Kongo und aus Indien, gibt es eine bemerkenswerte Auswahl an Teppichen, darunter antike Teppiche und schwer aufzutreibende, handgewobene Stücke aus dem Orient.

Plus d'un tiers des objets vendus dans ce vrai « souk » à meubles et décoration est issu de la production équitable, avec une attention spéciale portée sur les aspects sociaux du pays de production et sur la protection de l'environnement. En plus des objets d'art du Congo ou d'Inde, vous trouverez une remarquable sélection de tapis, allant de l'antiquité aux rares tapis d'Orient tressés à la main.

En este bazar con clase, más de dos tercios de los productos a la venta son producidos de manera sostenible, teniendo en cuenta las circunstancias sociales del país productor y respetando el medio ambiente. El inventario abarca muebles y objetos de decoración para el hogar. Aparte de las piezas de arte provenientes del Congo y de la India se puede apreciar también una considerable selección de alfombras que incluye antigüedades y telas orientales tejidas a mano difíciles de encontrar.

Apple Store 5th Avenue

767 5th Avenue
New York, NY 10153
Midtown East
Phone: +1 / 212 / 3 36 14 40
www.apple.com

Opening hours: Mon–Sun 24 hours
Products: Electronics
Subway: N, R, W at 5th Avenue
Map: No. 27

Russell James' Special Tip
Shaped like a gleaming cube, this store never closes so you can buy a new iPod at 5 a.m.

From the glass cube entranceway to the round-the-clock hours of operation, the Apple store on the corner of Central Park South and Fifth feels like a glimpse into the future. It is also perhaps the most cosmopolitan locale in the entire city. Luckily, iPod, iPhone and iBook are the same in every language.

Vom Glaskubus am Eingang bis hin zu den 24-Stunden-Öffnungszeiten erscheint der Apple Store an der Ecke von Central Park South und der Fifth Avenue wie ein Blick in die Zukunft. Vielleicht handelt es sich sogar um den kosmopolitischsten Ort der ganzen Stadt. Glücklicherweise heißen iPod, iPhone und iBook in jeder Sprache gleich.

La boutique Apple situé au carrefour de Central Park South et de Fifth Avenue est un concept futuriste tant par son entrée en forme de cube de verre que par ses horaires d'ouverture (24 heures sur 24). C'est sans doute l'endroit le plus cosmopolite de toute la ville. Heureusement que iPods, iPhones et iBooks sont des termes universels.

Bien sea por la entrada de cristal en forma de cubo o por su horario de apertura las 24 horas del día, la tienda de Apple en la esquina del parque Central Park South con la Fifth Avenue nos permite echar una ojeada al futuro. Es posiblemente el establecimiento más cosmopolita de toda la ciudad. Por fortuna el iPod, el iPhone y el iBook tienen el mismo nombre en todos los idiomas.

de Vera

1 Crosby Street
New York, NY 10013
SoHo
Phone: +1 / 212 / 6 25 08 38
www.deveraobjects.com

Opening hours: Mon closed, Tue–Sat 11 am to 7 pm, Sun closed
Products: Antique/vintage furniture, jewelry
Subway: J, M, N, Q, R, W, Z, 6 at Canal Street
Map: No. 28

A luxe curiosity shop for the 21st century, it is hard to categorize de Vera. The proprietor, who opened the first de Vera in San Francisco in 1991, offers a curated selection that crosses centuries and continents. Antiques are mixed in with jewelry of his own design for a unique and awe-inducing shopping experience.

Ein luxuriöser Laden voller Kuriositäten inmitten des 21. Jahrhunderts. Es fällt schwer de Vera zu definieren. Der Inhaber, der den ersten de Vera 1991 in San Francisco eröffnet hat, bietet eine gepflegte Auswahl an Objekten aus den verschiedensten Jahrhunderten und aus allen Kontinenten. Ein Mix aus Antiquitäten und von ihm selbst designtem Schmuck bietet ein einzigartiges und erstaunliches Shopping-Erlebnis.

Un magasin de curiosités de luxe pour le 21ème siècle, il est difficile de classer De Vera dans une catégorie. Le propriétaire, qui a ouvert le premier De Vera à San Francisco en 1991, propose une sélection qui traverse les siècles et les continents. Les antiquités se mélangent aux bijoux dessinés par lui même, créant ainsi une expérience de shopping unique et merveilleusement enivrante.

Una lujosa tienda de curiosidades a la medida del siglo XXI. Es difícil categorizar el de Vera. El propietario, que abrió el primer de Vera en San Francisco en 1991, ofrece una exquisita selección que abarca diferentes siglos y continentes, y en la que las antigüedades se mezclan con joyas diseñadas por él mismo. Un lugar donde ir de compras que garantiza una experiencia única y asombrosa.

Dean & DeLuca

560 Broadway at Prince Street
New York, NY 10012
SoHo
Phone: +1 / 212 / 2 26 68 00
www.deandeluca.com

Opening hours: Mon–Fri 7 am to 8 pm, Sat–Sun 8 am to 8 pm
Products: Gourmet shops/produce, candy/chocolate, kitchen/tableware
Subway: N, R at Prince Street
Map: No. 29

Lydia Hearst's Special Tip
Dean & Deluca is spacious, immaculate and a quiet place to sit and enjoy a quality cup of fresh coffee.

The essential SoHo supermarket. When it opened in 1977, Dean & DeLuca revolutionized the way New Yorkers ate. Its owners sought to bring fresh international products to the city's gourmets, who were starved for quality products. D&D was among the country's first importers of balsamic vinegar.

Der unabdingbare Supermarkt SoHos. Mit der Eröffnung 1977, revolutionierten Dean & DeLuca die kulinarischen Gewohnheiten der New Yorker. Die Inhaber waren bestrebt den Feinschmeckern der Stadt, die nach Qualitätsprodukten hungerten, internationale und frische Produkte zu bieten. D&D gehörten zu den ersten Importeuren von Balsamico-Essig des Landes.

Le supermarché indispensable de SoHo. A son ouverture en 1977, Dean & DeLuca ont révolutionné la façon de manger des new-yorkais. Les propriétaires ont voulu apporter des produits frais du monde entier aux fines papilles de la ville qui manquaient terriblement de produits de qualité. D&D furent les premiers à importer du vinaigre balsamique dans le pays.

El supermercado imprescindible del SoHo. Al abrir sus puertas en 1977, el Dean & DeLuca revolucionó las costumbres culinarias de los habitantes de Nueva York. Sus propietarios aspiraban a ofrecer productos frescos internacionales a los gourmet de la ciudad, que pedían a gritos productos de calidad. D&D se cuenta entre los primeros importadores de balsámico de todo el país.

NICARAGUAN
MARAGOGIPE
100% ARABICA BEANS
ROAST: OR

THE MARAGOGIPE "ELEPHANT BEAN"
IS ONE ONLY. LARGER THAN ANY OTHER.
COFFEE BEAN. NICKED FROM NICARAGUA
THIS COFFEE - WELL BALANCED AND MILD WITH
PRONOUNCED ACIDITY. BALANCED LOW ROAST.
WITH A HINT OF FINE FRUITY FLAVOR.

$12/LB

BREAKFAST BLEND
ROAST: MILD   BODY: MEDIUM-FULL

DELICATE & PLEASANTLY TANGY, WITH SWEET
NOTES OF CARAMEL.
FINISHES WITH A HINT OF WARM FUDGE.

$12/LB

DEAN & DELUCA
ARABIAN MOCHA
INDONESIAN JAVA
ROAST: MILD

EXCEPTIONALLY RICH WITH HINTS OF VA.
& ROASTED NUTS. MOCHA BEANS A.
A DELIGHTFUL COMPLEXITY TO THE SMC
AND HEAVY BODIED JAVA.

$12/LB

F·A·O Schwarz

767 5th Avenue at 58th Street
New York, NY 10153
Midtown East
Phone: +1 / 212 / 6 44 94 00
www.fao.com

Opening hours: Mon–Wed 10 am to 7 pm, Thu–Sat 10 am to 8 pm, Sun 11 am to 6 pm
Products: Toys
Subway: N, R, W at 5th Avenue
Map: No. 30

Lydia Hearst's Special Tip
This toy store is legendary! With a Candy Bar on the second floor and Milkshake Cafe on the first, it's fun for the whole family.

Everyone is a kid again at this world famous toy emporium. From its menagerie of life-sized stuffed animals to the giant floor piano made famous in the movie *Big*, it is hard to resist having fun at F·A·O Schwarz. The old-fashioned ice cream shop and candy store is a sweet-tooth's fantasy come to life.

Angesichts dieses weltbekannten Spielzeugwarenhauses wird jeder wieder zum Kind. Von einer ganzen Bandbreite lebensgroßer, ausgestopfter Plüschtiere bis hin zu dem Riesenklavier, das durch den Film *Big* berühmt wurde, ist die Auswahl groß und man kann gar nicht anders, als im F·A·O Schwarz Spaß zu haben. Der altmodische Eiscreme- und Süßwarenladen ist ein wahrgewordener Traum einer jeden Naschkatze.

Tout le monde redevient enfant dans cet empire du jouet connu dans le monde entier. De sa ménagerie d'animaux en peluche à taille réelle à son piano géant rendu célèbre par le film *Big*. Il est difficile de ne pas s'amuser chez F·A·O Schwarz. Le glacier et magasin de bonbons comme autrefois ne laissera pas les gourmands indifférents.

Cada visitante vuelve a ser niño dentro de este gran almacén de juguetes. Ya sea por su colección de peluches a tamaño real o por el piano gigantesco en el suelo, famoso desde la película *Big*, es difícil resistirse a la diversión en F·A·O Schwarz. El puesto de helados a la antigua y la tienda de golosinas convierten en realidad todos los sueños de los amantes del dulce.

SHOPS · F·A·O Schwarz   143

MoMA Design and Book Store

11 West 53rd Street
New York, NY 10019
Midtown West
Phone: +1 / 212 / 7 08 97 00
momastore.org

Opening hours: Mon–Thu 9:30 am to 6:30 pm, Fri 9:30 am to 9 pm, Sat–Sun 9:30 am to 6:30 pm
Products: Books, design objects, art reproductions
Subway: E, V at Fifth Avenue-53rd Street
Map: No. 31

While away an afternoon thumbing through the beautiful art and photography books at the MoMA Design and Book Store, adjacent to the museum. High design gadgets, toys and gifts are also on offer here and at the sister store across the street, which focuses on design including unique jewelry and fashions.

Warum nicht am Nachmittag ein wenig die Zeit vertrödeln und in den wunderschönen Kunst- und Fotografiebüchern des MoMA Design and Book Store direkt neben dem Museum stöbern? Es gibt hier, wie auch in der Filiale auf der anderen Straßenseite, die sich vor allem auf Design einzigartiger Schmuck- und Kleidungsstücke spezialisiert hat, hochwertige Designspielereien, Spielzeug und Geschenkartikel.

Passez une après midi à feuilleter des livres magnifiques sur l'art et la photographie dans la librairie du MoMA jouxtant le musée. De l'autre coté de la rue, le magasin très orienté design avec des bijoux uniques vous propose aussi des gadgets très design, des jouets et des cadeaux.

Disfrute de una tarde agradable ojeando los preciosos libros de arte y fotografía en la tienda MoMa Design and Book Store contigua al Museo de Arte Moderno. Tanto aquí, como en la segunda filial al otro lado de la calle, centrada sobre todo en la venta de joyería y moda única, se ofrecen artilugios de diseño, juguetes y regalos.

moss

150 Greene Street
New York, NY 10012
SoHo
Phone: +1 / 212 / 2 04 71 00
www.mossonline.com

Opening hours: Mon–Sat 11 am to 7 pm, Sun noon to 6 pm
Products: Furniture, accessories
Subway: N, R at Prince Street
Map: No. 32

Design addicts and newbies alike should pay a visit to this SoHo headquarters for all things design. For design fans, the draw is clear but the uninitiated too will find much to marvel at; iconic contemporary furniture, industrial design and limited edition studio pieces—all on display.

Designsüchtige und Neulinge auf diesem Gebiet sollten gleichermaßen den Hauptsitz für Design aller Art in SoHo besuchen. Für Designfans ist klar, warum sich der Besuch lohnt, aber auch Uneingeweihte werden hier viel zu bestaunen haben: Zu sehen gibt es zeitgenössische Kultmöbel, Industriedesign und limitierte Einzelstücke.

Les accros et les novices en design doivent faire un tour dans ce quartier général de SoHo en matière de design en tout genre. C'est un endroit très attrayant non seulement pour les amateurs de design, mais aussi pour les non initiés qui y trouveront de quoi les émerveiller. Œuvres de design industriel et éditions limitées de studio – toutes en exposition permanente.

Tanto los iniciados en el diseño como los principiantes deberían echar un vistazo a este cuartel general de todo lo diseñado en el SoHo. La atracción que el moss genera en los adeptos al diseño es comprensible, pero también el resto de los mortales podrá gozar con las creaciones que aquí se concentran: icónicos muebles contemporáneos, diseño industrial y piezas de edición limitada en exposición.

SHOPS . moss 149

Patricia Field

302 Bowery
New York, NY 10012
East Village
Phone: +1 / 212 / 9 66 40 66
www.patriciafield.com

Opening hours: Mon–Thu 11 am to 8 pm, Fri–Sat 11 am to 9 pm, Sun 11 am to 7 pm
Products: Clothing, accessories
Subway: F, V at Lower East Side-2nd Avenue, 6 at Bleecker Street
Map: No. 33

Lydia Hearst's Special Tip
Filled with models, celebrities and hipsters, this is an edgy cult landmark.

Perhaps most famous as the woman behind the fabulously concocted outfits that appeared in *Sex and the City*, Patricia Field has been dressing New York scenesters since the opening of her first Greenwich Village boutique in 1966. The store carries fun, original costume jewelry, clothes and accessories.

Vielleicht ist sie am bekanntesten dafür, die Frau zu sein, die hinter den fabelhaft zusammengestellten Outfits von *Sex and the City* steckt. Patricia Field hat die New Yorker Szene jedoch schon seit der Eröffnung ihrer ersten Greenwich Village Boutique 1966 eingekleidet. Im Geschäft findet man lustigen, originellen Modeschmuck, Kleidung und Accessoires.

Plus connu comme la femme étant derrière les tenues très élaborées apparaissant dans *Sex and the City*, Patricia Field habille les acteurs de la scène new-yorkaise depuis l'ouverture de sa première boutique à Greenwich Village en 1966. On y trouve des bijoux pour costumes, des vêtements et accessoires à la fois fantaisistes et originaux.

Quizás conocida en todo el mundo como la mujer tras los fabulosos vestuarios de la serie *Sexo en Nueva York*, Patricia Field lleva vistiendo a los adeptos a la moda desde la apertura de su primera tienda en Greenwich Village en 1966. Esta boutique ofrece bisutería, ropa y accesorios tan divertidos como originales.

PATRI
PATRICIA FIELD
PATRICIA FIELD
パトリシア
フィールド
HELLO KITTY

Strand Bookstore

828 Broadway at 12th Street
New York, NY 10003
Phone: +1 /212 / 4 73 14 52
www.strandbooks.com

Opening hours: Mon–Sat 9:30 am to 10:30 pm, Sun 11 am to 10:30 pm
Products: Books
Subway: N, R, Q, W, 4, 5, 6, L at Union Square
Map: No. 34

Lydia Hearst's Special Tip
On more than one occasion I have found myself browsing their vast collection of new and used books.

With "18 miles of books" this is a bibliophile's paradise. Used, new, out-of-print, and rare books cover the walls at this hallowed institution. It houses the city's largest rare book collection and, since 1927, has been the place to find tomes on any topic, particularly art, design and photography.

Mit seinen „18 Meilen an Büchern" ist dies ein Paradies für alle Buchliebhaber. Gebrauchte Bücher, neue Bücher und Bücher, die nicht mehr aufgelegt werden oder selten sind, türmen sich entlang der Wände dieser „geheiligten Institution" auf, die die größte Raritätensammlung der Stadt beherbergt und seit 1927 genau der richtige Ort ist, um Werke zu jedem Thema, besonders aber um Kunst-, Design- und Fotobände zu finden.

Avec « 18 miles de livres » c'est un paradis pour les bibliophiles. Neufs, d'occasion, épuisés ou rares, tous les livres tapissent les murs de cette institution sacrée. Elle renferme la plus grande collection de livres rares de la ville et depuis 1927 on y trouve chaque tome sur n'importe quel sujet, plus spéciale-ment sur l'art, le design et la photographie.

Con sus "18 millas de libros", el Strand Bookstore es un paraíso para cualquier amante de la lectura. Las paredes de esta consagrada institución están cubiertas de libros nuevos y de segunda mano, vo-lúmenes que ya no se editan y otros difíciles de encontrar. Esta librería contiene la colección de libros antiguos, raros y no catalogados más amplia de la ciudad y, desde 1927, es el lugar idóneo para encontrar libros sobre cualquier tema, pero sobre todo de arte, diseño y fotografía.

Takashimaya

693 5th Avenue
New York, NY 10022
Midtown
Phone: +1 / 212 / 3 50 01 00
www.takashimaya-ny.com

Opening hours: Mon–Sat 10 am to 7 pm, Sun noon to 5 pm
Products: Beauty supplies, furniture, clothing, accessories
Subway: E, V at 5th Avenue-53rd Street
Map: No. 35

This seven-level Japanese department store is located on Fifth Avenue. Offering sublime designs in menswear, womenswear, home and beauty, Takashimaya is an inspirational stop for memorable gifts and refined, distinctive style. Also worth a stop is The Tea Box, the restaurant and teashop on the store's lower level.

Dieses siebenstöckige japanische Kaufhaus befindet sich in der Fifth Avenue. Es gibt hier hochwertige Designermode für Männer und Frauen, Haushaltswaren und Kosmetikprodukte. Im Takashimaya findet man unvergessliche Geschenke und kultivierten, unverkennbaren Stil, der fähig ist, zu begeistern. Auch The Tea Box, das Restaurant und Teegeschäft im Untergeschoss, ist einen Besuch wert.

Ce grand magasin Japonais sur sept étages est situé sur Fifth Avenue. Takashimaya qui présente de sublimes designs pour la mode homme/femme, la maison et la beauté est une halte stimulante pour trouver des cadeaux inoubliables et raffinés de style exclusif. Vous pourrez aussi faire une pause au « Tea Box », le restaurant et la boutique de thé situé au sous-sol du magasin.

Este centro comercial japonés de siete plantas ubicado en la Fifth Avenue ofrece moda para hombre y mujer, artículos de decoración y productos de belleza de diseño sublime. Takashimaya es además una parada obligatoria cuando se trata de buscar regalos especiales u objetos de un estilo sofisticado y distintivo. El restaurante y salón de té The Tea Box en la primera planta también merece una visita.

TRAVELOGUES

Tribeca Issey Miyake

119 Hudson Street at North Moore
New York, NY 10013
TriBeCa
Phone: +1 / 212 / 226 0100
www.tribecaisseymiyake.com

Opening hours: Mon–Sat 11 am to 7 pm, Sun noon to 6 pm
Products: Clothing
Subway: 1 at Franklin Street
Map: No. 36

Chaos à la Frank Gehry rules supreme at the TriBeCa flagship. His titanium tornado sculpture holds court while the store itself offers all things Issey Miyake including the current menswear and womenswear collections as well as other lines like Pleats Please, Haat and Cauliflower and signature fragrances and accessories.

Im TriBeCa Flaggschiff-Store herrscht ein Chaos à la Frank Gehry. Seine Tornado-Skulptur aus Titan hält Hof, während alles was Issey Miyake zu bieten hat, einschließlich der laufenden Modekollektionen für Männer und Frauen sowie anderer Produktlinien wie Pleats Please, Haat und Cauliflower, Düfte und Accessoires der Firma, hier zu finden ist.

Le chaos selon Frank Gehry règne sur cet emblème du TriBeCa. Sa sculpture d'une tornade en titane trône à l'entrée tandis que dans le magasin on retrouve tout Issey Miyake, même sa collection homme et femme actuelle, d'autres lignes comme Pleats Please, Haat et Cauliflower ainsi que des grands parfums et accessoires de marque.

El caos al estilo Frank Gehry reina en la tienda de referencia de Issey Miyake en TriBeCa. Su tornado esculpido en titanio constituye el centro de atención y a su alrededor se exponen todos los objetos de la marca, incluyendo las colecciones actuales de hombre y mujer, otras líneas de producto como Pleats Please, Haat o Cauliflower, y perfumes y accesorios de la firma.

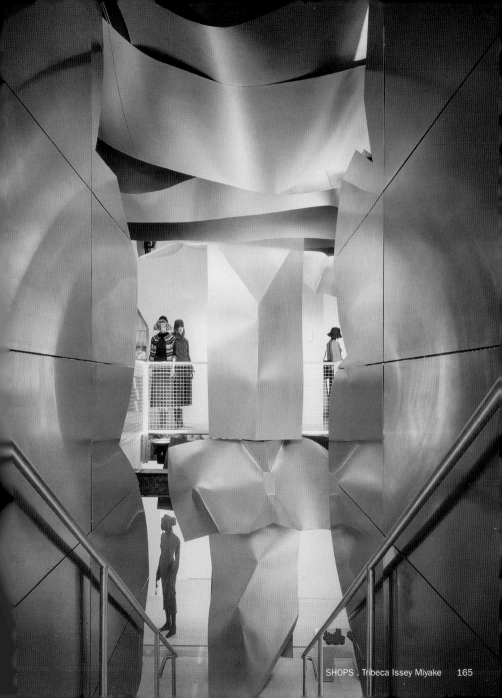

UNIQLO

546 Broadway
New York, NY 10012
SoHo
Phone: +1 / 917 / 2 37 88 11
www.uniqlo.com

Opening hours: Mon–Sat 10 am to 9 pm, Sun 11 am to 8 pm
Products: Clothing
Subway: N, R at Prince Street
Map: No. 37

Russell James' Special Tip
Stock up on cheap, chic fashions at this Japanese import's sprawling two-floor clothing store.

Japanese purveyor of cut-rate cashmere, the SoHo branch has become a secret weapon for budget conscious hipsters. Denim, trendy one-off pieces and the ubiquitous two-ply knits are on colorful display while Terry Richardson-shot ads and ongoing collaborations with artists and musicians add to the brand's cache.

Mit der Filiale in SoHo ist der japanische Lieferant extrem günstiger Qualitäts-Kaschmirware zur Geheimwaffe aller preisbewussten Hipster geworden. Es gibt Bekleidung aus Denim, trendige Einzelstücke und die allgegenwärtigen doppeltgewebten Strickwaren in allen Farben, während die Werbefotos von Terry Richardson und die Zusammenarbeit mit Künstlern und Musikern das ihre zur Note der Marke hinzutun.

Fournisseur japonais d'incroyable cachemire de qualité tout à fait abordable. Le magasin de SoHo est devenu une arme secrète pour les victimes de la mode qui font attention à leur budget. Denim, pièces de séries limitées de designers et autres omniprésents articles en laine 2 fils sont exposés sur des présentoirs chamarrés. Les photos publicitaires de Terry Richardson et les collaborations actuelles avec artistes et musiciens ajoutent au cachet de la marque.

La sucursal que esta empresa japonesa proveedora de cachemir de calidad a precios asequibles posee en el SoHo, se ha convertido en un arma secreta para los adeptos a la moda que miran también por su bolsillo. Aquí se exponen piezas de vaquero únicas y a la última, así como los omnipresentes géneros de punto de hilo de dos hebras en alegres colores. Las fotografías publicitarias de Terry Richardson que adornan las paredes y las continuas colaboraciones con artistas y músicos forman también parte del patrimonio de esta marca.

1980
THE NEW YORK AQUARIUM OPENS A
90,000 GALLON SHARK TANK

1940
THE PARACHUTE JUMP,
STANDING 277 FEET TALL,
IS RELOCATED FROM
THE 1939 WORLD'S FAIR
TO STEEPLECHASE PARK

"IF PARIS IS FRANCE,
CONEY ISLAND, BETWEEN
JUNE AND SEPTEMBER,
IS THE WORLD."
—GEORGE TILYOU

HIGHLIGHTS

American Museum of Natural History

Central Park West and 79th Street
New York, NY 10024
Phone: +1 / 212 / 7 69 51 00
www.amnh.org

Opening hours: Open daily 10 am to 5:45 pm, closed Thanksgiving and Christmas Day
Subway: B, C to 81st Street
Map: No. 38

From the hall of dinosaurs, presided over by an awe-inspiring Tyrannosaurus Rex, to the spooky dioramas showing underwater life, this museum is well worth a visit, with or without kids. The Hayden Planetarium is state of the art and the IMAX theater features science-themed films.

Von der Dinosaurierausstellung, deren Mittelpunkt ein erstaunlicher Tyrannosaurus Rex ist, bis hin zu den schaurigen Dioramen der Unterwasserwelt, ist dieses Museum wirklich einen Besuch wert, und zwar mit und ohne Kinder. Das Hayden Planetarium ist hochmodern und im IMAX Kino werden Filme zu wissenschaftlichen Themen gezeigt.

De son hall de dinosaures, avec à sa tête le majestueux Tyrannosaurus Rex, jusqu'à ses dioramas effrayants qui expliquent la vie aquatique, ce musée vaut vraiment le détour, avec ou sans enfants. Le Hayden Planétarium est ultramoderne et des films scientifiques sont projetés dans le cinéma IMAX.

Bien sea por su sala de los dinosaurios, presidida por un impresionante *tyrannosaurus rex*, o por los dioramas fantasmales que muestran la vida bajo el agua, este museo merece una visita –con o sin niños. El Hayden Planetarium hace gala de una tecnología punta y el cine IMAX ofrece filmes sobre temas científicos.

Brooklyn Bridge

Subway: A, C at High Street (Brooklyn); 4, 5, 6 at Brooklyn Bridge-City Hall
Map: No. 39

On a nice day, few city experiences rival a scenic walk across the Brooklyn Bridge. One of the world's largest suspension bridges, it leads into Brooklyn's Dumbo, a neighborhood known for its high-ceilinged loft spaces, expat Manhattanite families and cutting edge tech firms and design studios.

An einem schönen Tag können nur wenige Dinge, die die Stadt zu bieten hat, mit einem landschaftlich reizvollen Spaziergang über die Brooklyn Bridge mithalten. Die Brooklyn Bridge, eine der größten Hängebrücken der Welt, führt nach Dumbo, in ein Viertel, das bekannt ist für seine Lofts mit hohen Decken, in denen sich wohlhabende, aus Manhattan ausgewanderte Familien sowie hochmoderne Technologieunternehmen und Designstudios niedergelassen haben.

Lors d'une belle journée en ville, peu de choses valent une balade sur le Pont de Brooklyn, l'un des plus grands pont suspendu au monde. Il mène au quartier de Dumbo à Brooklyn, un quartier connu pour ses lofts à hauts plafonds, un quartier qui abrite des familles « expatriés » de Manhattan, des entreprises de pointe et des studios de design.

Hay pocas actividades en esta ciudad que puedan competir con un pintoresco paseo por el Puente de Brooklyn en un día despejado. Este es uno de los puentes colgantes más grandes del mundo y conduce directamente al barrio Dumbo, cuyo paisaje queda marcado por sus apartamentos de techos altos, ocupados por familias bien situadas de expatriados residentes en Manhattan, empresas vanguardistas de tecnología y estudios de diseño.

Bryant Park

Between 40th and 42nd Street and 5th and 6th Avenue
New York, NY 10018
www.bryantpark.org

Opening hours: 7 am daily, closing hours vary
Subway: 7 at 5th Avenue-Bryant Park, B, D, F, V at 42nd Street-Bryant Park
Map: No. 40

Bryant Park provides a bucolic patch of green in the midst of the city's densest neighborhood. A myriad of activities from Petanque and Tai Chi classes are offered during the warmer months and ice skating at the park's rink "The Pond" is offered during the fall and winter seasons. Workers from surrounding office buildings take advantage of the park's tables and chairs for outdoor lunches in nice weather.

Der Bryant Park ist ein idyllischer grüner Fleck inmitten des am dichtesten bewohnten Viertels. In den Sommermonaten werden unzählige Kurse von Petanque bis zu Tai Chi geboten, im Herbst und Winter kann man auf der Eisbahn „The Pond" Schlittschuh laufen. Angestellte der umliegenden Büros nutzen bei gutem Wetter gern die Gelegenheit, die Mittagspause an den Tischen und Bänken im Park zu genießen.

Bryant Park est un oasis de verdure bucolique situé au beau milieu d'un des quartiers les plus den-sément peuplés de la ville. Vous pourrez vous adonnez à une myriade d'activités comme la Pétanque, des cours de Tai Chi pendant la saison estivale et du patin à glace sur la patinoire du parc, « The Pond » (L'Étang), pendant la saison hivernale. Les employés de bureau des sociétés aux alentours profitent des tables et des chaises mises à leur disposition pour manger dehors dès que les beaux jours sont là.

El parque Bryant Park constituye una idílica franja verde en mitad del barrio más poblado de Nueva York. Durante los meses de verano el parque se presta a gran cantidad de actividades de ocio, que van desde la petanca hasta las clases de Tai-Chi. En los meses de invierno y otoño se puede patinar sobre hielo en el lago "The Pond". En los días despejados, los empleados de las oficinas cercanas aprovechan las mesas y sillas del parque para almorzar al aire libre.

Coney Island

Brooklyn, NY

Subway: D, F, N, Q to Coney Island
Map: No. 41

Vestiges of a bygone New York can still be found on this oceanfront strip, known for its amusement park rides and carnivalesque atmosphere. Burlesque shows, the famous wooden Cyclone rollercoaster, Nathan's hot dogs, the Mermaid Parade and the aquarium are some of the area's unique draws.

An diesem Abschnitt am Meer, der berühmt ist für seinen Vergnügungspark und die karnevaleske Atmosphäre, gibt es immer noch Überbleibsel eines New Yorks vergangener Zeiten. Variétévorstellungen, die berühmte Holzachterbahn Cyclone, Nathans Hotdogs, die Meerjungfrauen-Parade und das Aquarium sind einige der einzigartigen Anziehungspunkte.

On retrouve le passé de New York sur cette bande de terre au bord de l'océan connue pour son parc d'attraction, son ambiance de carnaval et ses spectacles burlesques. Le fameux Cyclone, grand huit en bois, les hot-dogs de Nathan, la parade des sirènes et l'aquarium sont quelques exemples d'attraction de l'endroit.

Todavía se pueden encontrar vestigios de la ciudad de Nueva York de antaño en esta franja frente al mar, conocida por su parque de atracciones y su atmósfera carnavalesca. Entre las principales atracciones de la zona se cuentan los espectáculos de tintes burlescos, la famosa montaña rusa de madera Cyclone, los perritos calientes de Nathan, el Desfile de las Sirenas y el acuario.

Statue of Liberty

Liberty Island, NY Harbor
www.nps.gov/stli

Opening hours: Mon–Sun 9 am to 5 pm except Dec 25th
Map: No. 42

Located on a 12 acre island in New York Harbor, the 'Statue of Liberty Enlightening the World' was a gift of friendship from the people of France to the people of the United States and is a universal symbol of freedom and democracy. Designed by Frédéric Bartholdi, the Statue of Liberty was dedicated on October 28, 1886, and designated as a National Monument in 1924.

Die Freiheitsstatue mit der offiziellen Bezeichnung „Statue of Liberty Enlightening the World" auf der 49.000m² großen Insel im New Yorker Hafen war ein Freundschaftsgeschenk des französischen Volkes an das Volk der Vereinigten Staaten und ist ein universelles Symbol für Freiheit und Demokratie. Die von Frédéric Bartholdi entworfene Statue wurde am 28. Oktober 1886 eingeweiht und 1924 zum Nationaldenkmal erklärt.

Située sur une île de 5 hectares dans le port de New York, la Statue de la « Liberté illuminant le monde » fut un cadeau d'amitié du peuple français au peuple américain et demeure un symbole universel de liberté et de démocratie. Dessinée par Frédéric Bartholdi, la Statue de la liberté fut inaugurée le 28 octobre 1886 et fut désignée monument national en 1924.

Ubicada en una isla de 49.000 metros cuadrados en el puerto New York Harbor, la "Estatua de la Libertad Iluminando el Mundo" fue un regalo del pueblo francés a los estadounidenses y es un símbolo universal de la libertad y la democracia. El monumento fue diseñado por Frédéric Bartholdi y entregado el 28 de octubre de 1886. En 1924 la estatua fue declarada monumento nacional.

STATUE OF LIBERTY & ELLIS ISLAND

CIRCLE LINE

The Cloisters Museum and Gardens

99 Margaret Corbin Drive
Fort Tryon Park
New York, NY 10040
Phone: +1 / 212 / 9 23 37 00
www.metmuseum.org/cloisters

Opening hours: Mon closed, March–Oct Tue–Sun 9:30 am to 5:15 pm, Nov–Feb 9:30 am to 4:45 pm
Subway: A at 190th Street
Map: No. 43

Russell James' Special Tip
This leafy park provides a breathtaking Hudson River outlook, while the Cloisters' medieval art is stunning.

Located in the Fort Tryon Park, constructed in 1934 and opened to the public in 1938, The Cloisters is home to one of the best regarded collections of European medieval art and architecture in the country. It is a branch of the Metropolitan Museum of Art and comprises about 5000 works of art; highlights include the Unicorn Tapestries and an impressive collection of illuminated manuscripts.

The Cloisters befindet sich im Fort Tryon Park. 1934 erbaut und 1938 fürs Publikum geöffnet, beherbergt es heute eine der geschätztesten Sammlungen europäischer mittelalterlicher Kunst und Architektur des Landes. The Cloisters ist eine Abteilung des Metropolitan Museum of Art, die gut 5000 Kunstwerke unter ihrem Dach vereint; einige der Highlights sind die Wandteppiche „The Hunt of the Unicorn" und eine erlesene Sammlung von Werken der Buchmalerei.

A l'intérieur du Fort Tryon Park, construit en 1934 et ouvert au public en 1938, le « Cloisters » abrite une des plus belles collections d'art et d'architecture médiévale européenne du pays. C'est une annexe du Metropolitan Museum of Art qui expose environ 5 000 œuvres d'art ; à ne pas manquer : les tapisseries de « La chasse à la licorne » et une impressionnante collection de manuscrits illustrées.

Este museo, ubicado en el parque Fort Tryon Park, fue construido en 1934 y abrió sus puertas en 1938. Hoy almacena una de las mejores colecciones de arte y arquitectura medieval europea del país. El museo es una delegación del Museo Metropolitano de Arte y atesora unas 5.000 obras de arte. Las mayores atracciones son las tapicerías de unicornio y una colección impresionante de manuscritos ilustrados.

The Skyscraper Museum

39 Battery Place
New York, NY 10280
Phone: +1 / 212 / 9 68 19 61
www.skyscraper.org

Opening hours: Mon–Tue closed, Wed–Sun noon to 6 pm
Subway: 4, 5 at Bowling Green
Map: No. 44

Located on the southern tip of Manhattan, this Skidmore, Owings & Merrill-designed museum is devoted to the vertical structures that give New York its distinctive skyline. Exhibits celebrate the architecture, history and technology of tall buildings in New York and abroad.

Dieses von Skidmore, Owings & Merrill entworfene Museum an der Südspitze von Manhattan widmet sich den vertikalen Strukturen, die New Yorks charakteristische Skyline ausmachen. Die Ausstellungsstücke feiern die Architektur, Geschichte und Technologie aller hohen Gebäude New Yorks und der ganzen Welt.

Situé à la pointe sud de Manhattan, ce musée désigné par Skidmore, Owings et Merrill est dédié à ces structures verticales qui donnent à New York sa ligne d'horizon si unique. Les modèles d'exposition célèbrent l'architecture, l'histoire et la technologie de tous les gratte-ciel construits à New York ou ailleurs dans le monde.

Ubicado en la punta sur de Manhattan, este museo diseñado por Skidmore, Owings & Merrill está dedicado a las estructuras verticales que otorgan a Nueva York su distintiva silueta. Sus exposiciones rememoran la arquitectura, historia y tecnología de los grandes edificios de Nueva York y el extranjero.

THE SKYSCRAPER MUSEUM
BOOKSTORE

Times Square

between 6th and 8th Avenues and 42nd and 47th Streets
New York, NY 10036
Midtown
www.timessquarenyc.org

Subway: 1, 2, 3, 7, N, Q, R, S, W
Map: No. 45

The most famous intersection of New York was renamed in 1904 after the "New York Times", which had its publishing headquarters there. Since the end of the 19th century, Times Square has been the city's major entertainment hub. It was majorly overhauled in the late 90s and today offers many options for family entertainment.

Der berühmteste Knotenpunkt von New York wurde 1904 nach der „New York Times", die ihren Verlagshauptsitz hier hatte, umbenannt. Seit Ende des 19. Jahrhunderts ist der Times Square das Zentrum des Entertainments der Stadt. Er wurde in den späten 90ern neu gestaltet und bietet Familien heute viele Alternativen der Freizeitgestaltung.

Le carrefour le plus célèbre de New York a changé de nom en 1904 en l'honneur du « New York Times » qui y avait ses quartiers généraux. Times Square est le centre festif de la ville depuis la fin du 19ème siècle. Times Square a été complètement rénové à la fin des années 90 et offre diverses activités pour toute la famille.

El cruce más famoso de Nueva York debe, desde 1904, su nombre al periódico "New York Times", cuyas oficinas generales se encontraban en este punto. Desde finales del siglo XIX, el Times Square ha sido el epicentro del entretenimiento de la ciudad. Tras algunos cambios fundamentales a finales de los 90, el Times Square ofrece hoy numerosas actividades de ocio y entretenimiento para las familias.

Top of the Rock Observation Deck

30 Rockefeller Plaza
New York, NY 10020
Phone: +1 / 212 / 6 98 20 00
www.topoftherocknyc.com

Opening hours: Mon–Sun 8 am to midnight
Subway: B, D, F, Q at Rockefeller Center
Map: No. 46

Russell James' Special Tip
Don't wait at the Empire State Building—these panoramic, 70th-floor views are just as dramatic.

When Rockefeller Center's observation deck reopened in 2005 after a 20-year hiatus, visitors were rewarded with breathtaking 360-degree panoramic views from the 70th floor. Another draw is a state-of-the-art multimedia exhibit on the history of Rockefeller Center and its construction.

Als 2005 die Terrasse des Rockefeller Centers nach 20 Jahren endlich wiedereröffnet wurde, wurden die Besucher für das lange Warten mit atemberaubenden 360-Grad Panoramablicken von der 70. Etage belohnt. Ein weiterer Anziehungspunkt ist eine ultramoderne Multimedia-Ausstellung über die Geschichte des Rockefeller Centers und seinen Bau.

Depuis que la plateforme d'observation du Rockefeller Center a ré-ouvert en 2005, après 20 ans de fermeture, les visiteurs peuvent enfin profiter de vues panoramiques époustouflantes de 360 degrés depuis le 70ème étage. Autre attraction : l'ultra moderne exposition multimédia sur l'histoire du Rockefeller Center et de sa construction.

Cuando en 2005, después de una tregua de 20 años, la plataforma de observación del Rockefeller Center volvió a abrir sus puertas al público, los visitantes de la planta 70 fueron premiados con una impresionante vista panorámica de 360 grados. Otra de las maravillas del edificio es la exposición multimedia de tecnología punta sobre la historia del Rockefeller Center y su construcción.

ARRIVAL IN NEW YORK

By Plane

There are direct flights from various European cities to the airports John F. Kennedy International Airport and Newark Liberty International Airport. The La Guardia Airport is mainly serving domestic air traffic.

Further information on the airports: www.panynj.gov

John F. Kennedy International Airport (JFK)

Phone: +1 / 718 / 2 44 44 44

JFK is situated in Queens; approx. 24 km (15 miles) from Midtown Manhattan. After passing customs and baggage claim, follow the Ground Transportation signs to continue your travel into the city. Off-peak travel times range between 40 and 60 mins by cab or bus. With the SuperShuttle you can reach any address as well as all hotels in Manhattan. It departs at least every 20 mins and a single trip costs $13–$22. You can register for the trip into the city at the Ground Transportation Desk, reservations for return trips should be made 24 hrs in advance. Phone: +1 / 212 / 2 58 38 26 or +1 / 800 / 258 38 26, www.supershuttle. com. The buses of the New York Airport Service go to Manhattan (Grand Central Station, Port Authority Bus Terminal, Penn Station), single trip $15, Phone: +1 / 212 / 8 75 82 00, www.nyairportservice.com. Trips by Air Train and Subway are more complicated and also take longer: change trains at the subway station Howard Beach to subway A or at Jamaica Station to subway E, J, Z or to the Long Island Rail Road. Total travel times range between 70 and 90 mins, single trip $7, you can only carry a limited amount of baggage. Cabs to Midtown Manhattan are $45 fixed price plus charges for bridges and tunnels as well as tips. Only use licensed yellow cabs!

Newark Liberty International Airport (EWR)

Phone: +1 / 973 / 9 61 60 00

This airport is situated approx. 26 km (16 miles) from Midtown Manhattan in New Jersey and less complex than JFK. After customs and baggage claim, follow the Ground Transportation signs to continue your trip into the city, off-peak travel times range between 40 and 60 mins. Bus transfer with SuperShuttle (see above for reservation and pricing information) or with Newark Liberty Airport Express every 15–30 mins to Manhattan (Port Authority Bus Terminal, Bryant Park, Grand Central Station), single trip $14, Phone: +1 / 800 / 6 69 00 51, www.coachusa.com. More complicated is traveling by Air Train or normal trains: change trains at Newark Liberty International Airport Train Station to NJ Transit or Amtrak direction Penn Station, single trip approx. $15. Cabs to Midtown Manhattan, $40–$60 plus road charge and tips as well as additional charges for rush hour or weekends, if applicable.

Flight Safety

There are strict safety requirements for hand luggage, e.g. for carrying liquids. The Transport Security Administration is authorized to open travelers' luggage without their permission, if necessary by force. Therefore, do not lock your luggage. Furthermore, custom authorities are allowed to check computers and data storage media without the necessity of concrete suspicious facts. For information on current regulations visit the website of the US embassy www.tsa.gov.

Immigration and Customs Regulations

Travel documents: Travelers need to have the correct travel documents and visas if necessary. Visas can be applied for at the American Consulate based in the country of origin.

Border control: Since January 2009, travelers of participating Visa Waiver countries need to fill out an online form at least 72 hours prior to their journey. https://esta.cbp.dhs.gov/esta. All other travelers should check their requirements to enter the country with their local US embassy. On check-in travelers already have to present either a booking confirmation for their hotel or provide details concerning the location of their initial accommodation. When entering the US, electronic fingerprints as well as an electronic portrait photo are taken from all visitors. Furthermore, you may be asked about your return ticket, the motivation for your trip and/or your domicile during your stay.

Customs: Adults 21 years and older are allowed to bring in 200 cigarettes or 50 cigars or 2 kg of tobacco as well as 1 l of alcohol and presents amounting to a value of $100. The import of comestibles is prohibited.

INFORMATION

Tourist Information

NYC & Company
810 Seventh Avenue New York,
NY 10019
Phone: +1 / 212 / 4 84 12 00
Fax: +1 / 212 / 2 45 59 43
www.nycgo.com
Mon–Fri 8:30 am to 6 pm, Sat+Sun 9 am to 5 pm

NYC Heritage Tourism Center
Corner Broadway/Park Row, south of City Hall Park.
Mon–Fri 9 am to 6 pm, Sat+Sun 10 am to 6 pm

Official Visitor Information Kiosk for Chinatown
Triangle at Canal/Walker/Baxter Street Sun–Fri 10 am to 6 pm, Sat 10 am to 7 pm

City Magazines
New York's most popular city magazine is **Village Voice**. It provides in-scene news and is published every Wed. It is available for free in many shops and clubs as well as in special boxes on the pavements. **Time Out New York** and **New York Magazine** are available every Wed respectively Mon at newspaper stands and offer a broad schedule of events, restaurant reviews, party recommendations and many more. The **New Yorker** is known for providing elaborate background essays. Furthermore, you can find information on current events in the supplements of the **New York Times**.

Websites

General
www.nyc.gov – Official site of New York City
www.nytimes.com – Web presence of the "New York Times", with news about the city, event calendar, online ticket service, restaurant search engine, cinema program, tips for travelers and many more

Going Out
City magazines and online travel guides offer information on restaurants, taverns, bars, events and many more on the Internet
newyork.citysearch.com
nymag.com
www.ny.com
www.timeoutny.com
www.villagevoice.com

Art and Culture
www.broadway.com – Program of Broadway shows

www.newyorker.com – Comprehensive art and culture program

www.nytheatre.com – Everything about the New York theater scene

Sports and Leisure

www.chelseapiers.com – Leisure and sport facility

www.nycgovparks.org – Sport and leisure time facilities in all parks of the city

www.skatecity.com/nyc – Skating in New York, with travel routes and maps

Map

www.newyork.citysam.de – Interactive city maps

Accommodation

www.1800usahotels.com/nycvisit/index.html – Hotel agency of the tourist information

newyork.citysearch.com – Online travel guide, hotel reservation etc.

www.nyhabitat.com – This site helps you to find apartments and Bed & Breakfast accommodations

www.priceline.com – hotel bookings with a feature to bid on a specified area and hotel category

Event calendars

www.nycvisit.com

newyork.citysearch.com

nymag.com

RECOMMENDED LITERATURE

Paul Auster

The New York Trilogy: "City of Glass", "Ghosts" and "Locked Room". Three elaborately constructed mystery fiction novels that describe the anonymity of big city life, the decay of social relationships and the loss of moral order.

Truman Capote

Breakfast at Tiffany's. The story of the mysterious, innocently wicked Holly Golightly, who is trying to find her luck in New York.

John Dos Passos

Manhattan Transfer. Multi-facetted picture of the New York of the early 20ies, where the pursuit of work, happiness and power is predominant.

F. Scott Fitzgerald

The Great Gatsby. One of the classics of American literature – a portrait of New York's monied nobility in the Roaring Twenties.

Tom Wolfe

The Bonfire of the Vanities. Tragical-comical bigcity novel about the Wall Street generation.

CITY TOURS

Sightseeing Tours

By Bus and Subway

An inexpensive way of seeing Manhattan is a trip with the **M 1 bus** from E 8th Street/4th Avenue (Mon–Fri also from South Ferry) to W 146th Street in Harlem and back. A trip with the **subway** to see the subterranean Manhattan is always worthwhile – not only when it is raining.

Gray Line

Phone: +1 / 800 / 6 69 00 51 and +1 / 212 / 4 45 08 48

www.graylinenewyork.com

The All Loops Tours have four different routes through Manhattan and Brooklyn with the red double-decker buses. The bus stops on demand at one of the 50 stops. A trip lasts between 2 and 3 hrs and buses depart every 30 mins at Times Square for **Downtown Loop** and the **Holiday Lights Tour**, from Gray Line Visitors Center (777 8th Avenue) for **Uptown Loop** and from South Street Seaport for the **Brooklyn Loop**. 48-hour ticket $44.

Boat Tours

Staten Island Ferry

A trip with the free ferry to Staten Island and back offers a great view on the Manhattan skyline and the Statue of Liberty. The ferry terminal is situated on Whitehall Street at the southern tip of Manhattan and ferries are leaving at least every 30 mins, duration of a single trip approx. 25 mins.

Circle Line

Phone: +1 / 212 / 5 63 32 00
www.circleline42.com
Boat trips of 75 mins and 2 hrs duration around the southern tip of Manhattan Island as well as a 3-hour island round trip. Departure from Pier 83 at the west end of 42nd Street. In summer various times a day, in winter less departures. Tickets $16–$31.

Sightseeing Flights

Helicopter round trips around the Statue of Liberty and over Downtown Manhattan. Flight times ranging between approx. 5–7 mins up to 30 mins, starting at $100/pers. Trial flight from 2 to 2.5 mins, $ 30/pers. Starting points: VIP Heliport (W 30th Street/12th Avenue), Downtown Manhattan Heliport (Pier 6 between South Street Seaport and Staten Island Ferry Terminal, Mon–Sat) and Paulus Hook Pier (Jersey City).

Helicopter Tours, Phone: +1 / 212 / 3 55 08 01
www.heliny.com

Liberty Helicopter Tours, Phone: +1 / 212 / 9 67 64 64 and +1 / 800 / 5 42 99 33
www.libertyhelicopters.com

Guided City Tours

Big Apple Greeter

1 Centre Street, 19th Floor, New York, NY 10007
Phone: +1 / 212 / 6 69 81 59
www.bigapplegreeter.org
People from New York provide a free guided tour for visitors through their city (max. 6 persons), duration 2 to 4 hrs. Registration via Internet, approx. 3–4 weeks in advance.

Big Onion Walking Tours

Phone: +1 / 212 / 4 39 10 90
www.bigonion.com
Competently guided walkabouts concentrating on special aspects and topics, e.g. immigration, gangs, etc., $15/pers.

Bike the Big Apple

Phone: +1 / 877 / 8 65 00 78
www.bikethebigapple.com
Guided bike tours through New York, duration 5–7 hours, length 8–15 miles, $70–$80/pers. incl. bike and helmet.

Harlem Heritage Tours

Phone: +1 / 212 / 2 80 78 88
www.harlemheritage.com
Thematic walkabouts through Harlem (e.g. about its history, gospel churches) as well as special musical tours (Salsa, Hip-Hop, Jazz), from $25/pers.

Insight Seeing

Phone: +1 / 718 / 4 47 16 45
www.insightseeing-tours.de

2- to 6-hour tours through Manhattan, Harlem, Bronx, Brooklyn, Queens and Staten Island, in English from $23/pers. Furthermore, individual tours, minimum duration 2 hrs, $75/hr.

Lookouts

Breathtaking views are offered to visitors of the Observation Deck of the **Empire State Buiding** (www.esbnyc.com) and from the Top of the Rock at **Rockefeller Center** (see above). Enjoy terrific views on the skyline of Manhattan from the **Staten Island Ferry** (see above), from the pavement leading over the **Brooklyn Bridge** or from **Roosevelt Island Tram**, an aerial cableway going over the East River (www.rioc.com). Virtual tours with unusual New York air perspectives can be undertaken at the **NYSkyride Cinema** at the Empire State Building (www.skyride.com).

TICKETS & DISCOUNTS

Ticket Offices

Order tickets for nearly all concerts, culture and sport events online or via phone at: **Ticketmaster**, Phone: +1 / 800 / 7 45 30 00, www.ticketmaster.com, phone service Mon–Fri 9 am to 9 pm, Sat to 8 pm, Sun to 6 pm **Telecharge**, Phone: +1 / 212 / 2 39 62 00, www.telecharge.com, 24-hour service

TKTS Theatre Centers

Discount tickets with reductions of 25 %, 35 % and 50 % for Broadway and Off-Broadway shows, for dance performances and musicals. Only available for shows and performances that take place on the respective day itself or matinees on the following day. Credit cards, cash or travelers checks accepted. All available tickets are announced via a display panel. www.tdf.org.

Points of sale: **TKTS Booth Times Square**, "under the red steps" 47th Street/Broadway, Mon–Sat 3 pm till 8 pm, Sun from 3 pm (evening shows), Wed and Sat 10 am till 2 pm, Sun 11 am till 3 pm (matinees).

TKTS Booth South Street Seaport, John Street/Front Street, Mon–Sat 11 am to 6 pm, Sun to 4 pm (evening shows), tickets for matinees only available one day in advance (Tue, Fri, Sat).

Downtown Brooklyn, 1 Metro Tech Center, Tue–Sat 11 am to 6 pm

Discounts

New York City Pass

50% entrance discount and no waiting times in the following locations: Empire State Building, MoMA, Guggenheim Museum, The Metropolitan Museum of Art and American Museum of Natural History as well as to a 2-hour Circle Line boat tour. Available at the Visitor Center, the participating companies or online at www.citypass.com, $74/pers.

Unlimited Ride MetroCard

Unlimited use of subway, Staten Island Railway and the city buses. Available amongst others at the Visitor Center, in hotels and at MetroCard vending machines, one-day ticket $7.50, seven-day ticket $25.

GETTING AROUND IN NEW YORK

Local Public Transport

Metropolitan Transportation Authority (MTA)

Phone: +1 / 718 / 3 30 12 34
www.mta.info
The fastest way to get around in New York is the

Subway. It operates on about 30 routes with high frequency around-the-clock. Staten Island is served by Staten Island Railway (SIR), Long Island by Long Island Rail Road (LIRR). Local trains stop at all stations, while the faster express trains only stop at the stations marked on the subway maps with white circles and ovals. In addition to the subway there is a dense **network of bus lines**. Buses commute from 6 am until about midnight every 5–15 mins. A single ticket for subway or bus is $2, for express buses $5, multiple-ride tickets with the rechargeable MetroCard, unlimited rides with the Unlimited Ride MetroCard. Available amongst others in subway stations, MetroCard vending machines and kiosks, single tickets can also be bought from the bus driver (make sure you pay the exact amount in coins as drivers do not return any change!). The network maps for the subways, trains and buses are available for download at the homepage of the Metropolitan Transportation Authority or for free in subway stations or buses.

Cabs

Phone: +1 / 212 / 3 02 82 94
Going by cab is relatively cheap in New York: $2.50 basic charge for the first 1/3-mile, $0.40 for every further 1/5-mile or for every 2 mins in case of traffic jam. Furthermore, additional charges for night trips from 8 pm–6 am, trips during rush hour, tunnel and bridge tolls have to be paid if applicable as well as a tip of 15–20 %. Normally, cabs are stopped by waving with the hand. When a cab is available the number on the roof is lighted, ordering a cab by phone is unusual. Only use licensed cabs – the yellow ones, that all are equipped with a taxi meter. Non-licensed cabs, so-called *gypsy cabs* most often do not dispose of insurance and claim higher charges.

FESTIVALS & EVENTS
This is just an excerpt from the program for the year.

Lunar New Year Celebration

End of Jan/beginning of Feb (at the first full moon after January 21), New Year's celebration in Chinatown with parades, dragon dances and fireworks (www.explorechinatown.com).

St. Patrick's Day Parade

Around March 17, grand parade on Fifth Avenue between 44th and 86th Street in honor of the Irish national saint (www.saintpatricksdayparade.com).

Great Five Boro Bike Tour

At the beginning of May, 42-miles bike tour through the five boroughs of New York City, accompanied by a festival (www.bikenewyork.org).

Museum Mile Festival

One Tuesday in early June, free admission to the nine big museums on Fifth Avenue as well as a street festival with live bands and entertainment (www.museummilefestival.org).

Shakespeare in the Park

Mid June–beginnings of July, Shakespeare performances on the open-air stage of the Delacorte Theater at Central Park, free admission, always starting at 8:30 pm, tickets can be obtained on the day of the performance at the Public Theater on Lafayette Street (Phone: +1 / 212 / 5 39 86 50, www.publictheater. org).

Central Park Summer Stage

Mid June–Mid Aug, concerts, dance performances, movie screenings and lectures on a stage in the middle of Central Park, various events per week, usually free admission (www.summerstage.org).

Downtown River to River Festival
Mid June–Sept, more than 500 cultural events in theaters and museums on squares and in parks in Lower Manhattan (www.rivertorivernyc.com).

Good Morning America Concert
Beginning of July–end of Aug, first-class pop concerts on the Upper Terrace in Bryant Park, free admission, starting at 7 am! (www.bryantpark.org).

New York Philharmonic in the Park
Mid July, open-air concerts of the Philharmonic Orchestra in Central Park and other green places in the city, with final fireworks, starting in each case at 8 pm (www.newyorkphilharmonic.org).

Sept 11th Anniversary
11th Sept, commemoration for the victims of the terrorist attacks on the World Trade Center with concerts, exhibitions and light show.

Greenwich Village Halloween Parade
Oct 31, nocturnal costume and torch procession between Spring Street / 22nd Street (www.halloween-nyc.com).

ING New York Marathon
Beginning of November, the biggest marathon in the world leads through the five boroughs of New York City (www.nycmarathon.com).

Lighting of the Rockefeller Center Christmas Tree
End of Nov/beginning of Dec, illumination of the big Christmas tree on Rockefeller Plaza.

New Year's Eve Ball
December 31, giant party starting in the early evening at Times Square with the famous Ball Drop from the top of the building One Times Square at 11.59 pm (www.timessquarebid.org).

USEFUL NOTES

Electricity
Voltage 110 volt. For electrical appliances you will need an adaptor.

Money
National currency: US-Dollar ($) 1 Dollar ($) = 100 Cents (ct) Exchange rates (as of late 2008): $1 = approx. € 0.80 or € 1 = approx. $1.30
Bank and credit cards: Credit cards and travelers checks are accepted nearly everywhere. With EC-/Maestro-Cards and pin number you can withdraw US dollars from bank machines and all other ATMs: pull the card through the card reader, enter your PIN-number and choose option "Withdrawal from Checking". Notes of 50 and 100 dollars are only changed reluctantly in shops.

Health Insurance
Medical consultations and hospital stays have to be paid right away. Because of the high costs for medical care, a travel health insurance is strongly recommended.

Emergency
Emergency Hotline: Phone: 911 (police, fire department)
Emergency Doctor: Phone: + 1 / 800 / 3 95 34 00
Hotline for Crime Victims: Phone: +1 / 212 / 5 77 77 77
New York Urgent Care Center: Phone: +1 / 212 / 7 37 12 12 (24-hour service, the doctors come directly to the hotel)

Opening Hours
Banks: Normally Mon–Fri 9 am to 3.30 pm, often Thu or Fri to 6 pm.
Shops: There is no store closing law in the USA.

Many shops are open 24/7. Jewish shops, mainly on the Lower East Side, are closed from Fri afternoon until Sat night.

Museums: Usually opened Tue–Sun 10 am to 5 pm, often opened until the evening once a week.

Restaurants: Upscale restaurants 11:30 am to 2 pm for lunch and 6 pm to 10 pm for dinner. Many taverns and restaurants are open throughout the day or even around the clock.

Smoking

Smoking is prohibited in public buildings, cabs, public transport vehicles, restaurants, bars and clubs. At hotels smokers should ask for a smoking room.

When to go

There is no specific season for traveling to New York—you can go there all year long. Summers can be very hot and sultry though. In July and Aug temperatures often reach 28°C. In Jan and Feb blizzards are likely to occur.

Safety

Today, New York is regarded to be the safest city in the USA. Nevertheless, the usual precautions should be taken. Especially around Times Square and other busy places, in Grand Central Station and at the Port Authority bus station pick pocketing can occur. At night you should avoid empty streets and parks. All subway lines are busy till late at night. It is recommended to wait in the off-hour waiting areas that are situated near the exits of the stations.

Telephone

Area Codes of New York: 212, 917, 646 (Manhattan) and 718, 347 (Brooklyn, Bronx, Queens, Staten Island). Dial 1 first

Within New York: 1 + area code + desired phone number

Calling from Abroad: +1 + desired phone number without 0

Calling from New York: country code + area code without 0 + desired phone number

Operator: national: dial 0, international: dial 00 (telephone exchange of distance and collect calls as well as in case of emergency)

Directory Assistance: Phone 411

Toll-free numbers: 1 + 800, 888, 866 or 877 + desired phone number. With a prepaid phone card you can also make international calls. The activation code is disclosed when calling the phone number on the card. Phone cards are available at newspaper kiosks or tourist information centers. Cell phones only work when they are equipped with triband technology. You can rent a cell phone for the time of your stay in New York, e.g. at the airport.

Tipping

In the United States service employees mainly live from the tips they get. Waiters and cab drivers receive a minimum tip of 15 % of the bill, most of the time you just double the tax. Chambermaids, porters, shoeshine boys and wardrobe attendants expect a tip of $1–2.

HUDSON
RIVER

20 18 9 14 17 22 13

Hudson Street

Canal Street

SOHO

32

1 36

TRIBECA

8

28

7

2

CHINA
TOWN

44

42

41

39

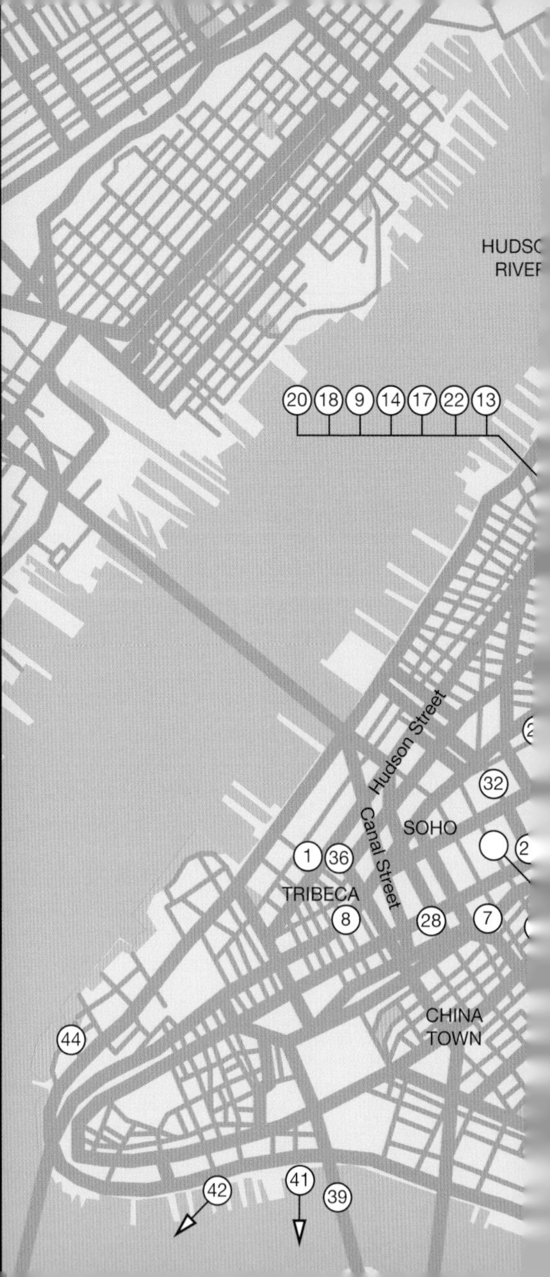

UPPER WEST SIDE

CENTRAL PARK

UPPER EAST SIDE

43

38

4

27 30

10

23 CHELSEA

45

6th Ave.

31 35

12

57th Street

Broadway

Lincoln Tunnel

W. 23rd Street

46

MIDTOWN

19 40

6

W. 34th Street

Park Ave.

W. 14th Street

16

First Ave.

Queens Midtown Tunnel

3 26

24

QUEENS

Union Square Park

34

adway
fayette

15 29 37

5

EAST VILLAGE

Houston Street

WER
T SIDE

EAST RIVER

BROOKLYN

Other titles by teNeues

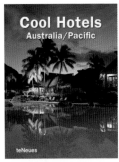

ISBN 978-3-8327-9309-8

ISBN 978-3-8327-9274-9

ISBN 978-3-8327-9237-4

ISBN 978-3-8327-9247-3

ISBN 978-3-8327-9234-3

ISBN 978-3-8327-9308-1

ISBN 978-3-8327-9243-5

ISBN 978-3-8327-9230-5

ISBN 978-3-8327-9248-0

Size: **15 x 19 cm**, 6 x 7½ in., 224 pp., **Flexicover**, c. 200 color photographs,
Text: English / German / French / Spanish / Italian
www.teneues.com

Other titles by teNeues

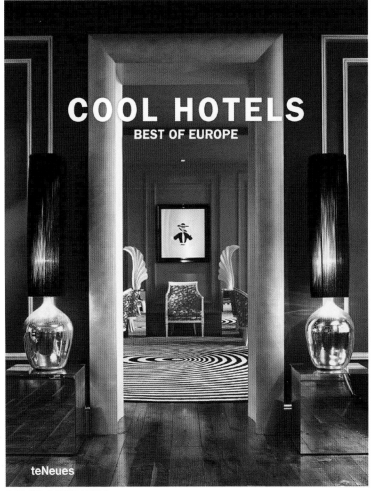

ISBN 978-3-8327-9235-0

Size: **25.6 x 32.6 cm**, 10 x 12⁷/₈ in., 396 pp., **Hardcover with jacket**, c. 650 color photographs,
Text: English / German / French / Spanish / Italian
www.teneues.com

teNeues' new Cool Guide series

ISBN 978-3-8327-9293-0

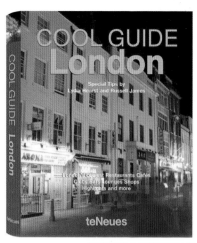

ISBN 978-3-8327-9294-7

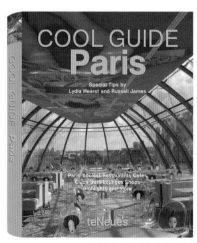

ISBN 978-3-8327-9295-4

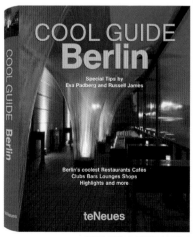

ISBN 978-3-8327-9296-1

Size: **15 x 19 cm**, 6 x 7 ½ in., 224 pp., **Flexicover**, c. 250 color photographs,
Text: English / German / French / Spanish
www.teneues.com